Six-String Stories

Mick Morris

To Matthew
with
best wishes
Mick Morris

Blue Tree Books, England

Independent Publishing Network

ISBN: 9781973398011

ACKNOWLEDGMENTS

Except for the personal contributions, I do not claim authorship or ownership of the quotes or stories themselves, though I take full responsibility for the organisation of the material and the personal views expressed.

Wherever possible I've named the source or contributor but it's in the nature of such things that many may be purely anecdotal. Some of them have been in circulation for many years and despite extensive research their provenance remains unknown. In the event of any errors or omissions coming to light, the author and publisher will be pleased to make any necessary corrections in future editions.

I'd like to thank the many friends and others who've contributed stories and quotes. Special thanks to David Kessel for allowing access to his memories of his father Barney Kessel and to Harvey Kubernik for permission to reproduce extracts from his `*Spectropop*' articles.

MAM

Introduction

I've been reading, writing and collecting stories about guitars and guitar players pretty much all my life. Some years ago, I put some of my favourites into a little book for the interest and amusement of my musician friends, but the collection has continued to grow and I thought an update was long overdue.

If it's made me aware of one thing, it is that a book like this can never truly be finished. Not only is new material surfacing all the time but whilst most guitar players love nothing better than to talk about their music, other guitarists and their passion for the instrument, there are a few notable exceptions and hence some surprising omissions which it would take another volume and a lot more research to rectify

Some of what follows may be familiar, most I hope will amuse and some facts I'm pretty sure will surprise.

MAM

November 2017

CONTENTS

1 Well, I never knew that

ABOUT THE GEETAR

Most of what you've probably been told about the origins of the guitar is almost certainly wrong. For example, it's often claimed that the guitar is a development of the ancient Greek instrument the kithara, but the kithara was a completely different type of instrument, a square-framed lap harp, or lyre. I find it not only hard but unnecessary to imagine how and why it metamorphosed into the guitar when there's a much more obvious candidate to hand. It seems far more likely to have developed from the tanbur, an ancient string instrument with a long, straight neck, small egg or pear-shaped body, arched or round back and a soundboard of wood or hide. The tanbur itself probably developed from the bowl harp, the bowed neck of which became straightened out to allow the strings to be pressed down in order to create more notes.

Even the word `guitar' is probably the wrong name for the instrument most of us play today. The `tar' part of the word comes from the ancient Sanskrit word for `string' and the prefix `gui' is meant to indicate the number of strings. Except that it doesn't.

The prefix element of the instrument name was originally a Sanskrit word as well but in its migration to English has traveled through other languages - first Persian, then Spanish via the Moors.

In Sanskrit, `dvi' means `two' which becomes `do' in modern Persian. Similarly `three' is `tri' in Sanskrit and `se' in Persian. The *dotar* therefore is a two-stringed instrument, still found in Turkestan. The *setar*, still found in Iran, originally had three strings but is known as the *sitar* in India despite many radical changes to the instrument. Which brings us back to the object of our curiosity. The Sanskrit word for four is `chatur', in Persian `char'. Via Spanish, *chartar* became *quittarra,* eventually anglicised to *guitar* .

Unsurprisingly perhaps there is also the *panchtar*, from Sanskrit `pancha' and Persian `panj', a five-stringed instrument played mostly in Afghanistan.

But, with only one more string to go, we seem to have run out of names. These guys I've got hanging on the wall mostly have six strings and they're not happy about being named after a four-stringed, 17th century Spanish antique I can tell you. So, welcome to the *sheshtar* (or should that be sixtar?)

Mick Morris (from the tutor book `Play Straight Away')

The Allman Brothers Band song, *`Jessica'* was written by Dickey Betts in tribute to Django Reinhardt. Dickey wanted to write a song that could be played using only two fingers. Django's remarkable achievement in overcoming his disability also inspired Tony Iommi to keep playing guitar after a factory accident cost him two fingertips.

Tal Farlow, one of the greatest guitarists of the 20th Century, was almost as famous for his reluctance to perform publicly as for his outstanding ability on the instrument. Despite being hugely talented, Tal valued other aspects of his life more highly than the music business and in 1958, aged only thirty-eight, went into musical semi-retirement and returned to his earlier career as a sign painter.

Over the next nearly twenty years, he resurfaced only occasionally to record and make sporadic appearances in local clubs. He made just one record as a leader between 1960 and 1975. He emerged a bit more often between 1976 and 1984, recording fairly regularly for Concord records before largely disappearing from public view again.

Link Wray's `Rumble' was written as an impromptu piece during a live TV show. Wray originally called it `Oddball'. It was changed to `Rumble' following a suggestion by Phil Everly who said it sounded rough, like a street fight.

By the way, `Rumble is an example of a very rare musical form, the eleven-and-a-half-bar blues!

In January 1948, Les Paul was involved in a serious car accident on Route 66 near Davenport, Oklahoma, the accident shattering his right arm and elbow. Doctors at the Wesley Presbyterian Hospital in Oklahoma City told him they couldn't rebuild the elbow in such a way as to restore full movement; his arm would remain permanently in whatever position they fixed it. The only other option was amputation. Paul instructed the surgeons to set his arm at an angle of just under 90 degrees, which he calculated would allow him to hold and play the guitar. It took him nearly a year and a half to recover.

Incidentally, Les Paul and Mary Ford were introduced to each other by guitar-playing, singing cowboy Gene Autry in 1946. At their wedding in 1949, Steve Miller's father was Les' best man. Later, Les became Steve's instructor, giving him his first guitar lessons.

The young Robbie Robertson received insider guitar advice from Buddy Holly. Robertson was just fourteen years old when he went to see Alan Freed's Revue tour in the fall of 1957. Fats Domino, Chuck Berry, the Everly Brothers and Frankie Lymon were all on the bill, but what Robertson was waiting to see were the headliners, Buddy Holly and the Crickets. After the show, Robertson pushed his way to the front of the stage and asked the 21-year-old singer-guitarist how he got his unique guitar sound.

"Here's the thing," Holly responded, much to Robertson's astonishment. "I got this Fender amp with two 12-inch speakers. I blew one of the speakers, and thought it sounded better, so I left it." "I couldn't believe it," he writes, "not only was Buddy Holly a genuinely nice guy, he was willing to reveal the kind of inside information I was hungry for."

Donovan taught the Beatles finger-picking techniques he had learned from listening to Bert Jansch's early albums. What Donovan taught them helped determine the sound of Lennon/McCartney originals such as Blackbird and Julia.

(quoted in Pete Paphides' article in The Guardian, Thursday 6 October 2011)

~~~~~~~~

Before achieving fame in his own right, Glen Campbell worked as a session musician. In the 1960s he worked with Bobby Darin, Ricky Nelson, The Monkees, Elvis Presley, Frank Sinatra, The Velvet Underground, Frankie Laine, The Association, Jan & Dean and The Mamas & the Papas. He was a touring member of The Beach Boys, filling in for an ailing Brian Wilson in 1964 and 1965. Among many other recordings, his guitar playing can be heard on 'Strangers in the Night' by Frank Sinatra, 'You've Lost That Lovin' Feelin'' by The Righteous Brothers and 'I'm a Believer' by The Monkees.

~~~~~~~~

Django Reinhardt's transition to the electric guitar has always been a bone of contention among his followers. Most of his fans

didn't approve and many are quite disparaging. But I'm not one of them. I'm one of the minority who regard Django's electric playing as quite superb.

But putting that to one side, there's always been something of a mystery surrounding why, when and where it came about.

It's often said that Django had not played an electric instrument before he went to the USA in October 1946 but a closer look reveals evidence to suggest otherwise.

> ➢ There is a brief article in the October 1945 issue of BMG magazine which states, "Django Reinhardt definitely uses an electric guitar these days. Details came from American banjoist Freddy Morgan who was compére for a Reinhardt show given under USO auspices recently at Nice, France."
>
> ➢ Photos, said to have been taken in late 1945, show Django with some crude amplification on his Selmer guitar. You can see the electric cord hanging from his guitar (perhaps using some kind of contact mic given to him by a US serviceman) and the amplifier on the chair in front of him.
>
> ➢ In an interview at the January 1946 recording sessions in London,

Django was asked for his views on `the electrically-amplified guitar' by Sam Adams of BMG. Django's response, quoted in the resulting article, *`I Meet Reinhardt',* was, "Yes, he had played the electric guitar for a few weeks, but did not like it as it would not produce what he described as the `human tone'."

➢ There is newsreel footage from May 1946 taken in a French club (The El Rodeo) which clearly shows Django playing a blonde Epiphone Zephyr arch-top electric through an Electar Zephyr Dreadnought amplifier. In the film, Eugene Vees can be seen sitting behind Django playing rhythm guitar. It is possible that the Epiphone belonged to Eugene who can be seen playing it himself in another film clip from two years after Django's death.

Stephane Grappelli tells a different story. He remembered that:

"Django first heard an electric guitar in 1946 or 1947 - I think it was at the Hackney Empire. Somebody brought in the guitar and it made a terrible noise - in those days electric guitars didn't sound as good as they do now. But Django was so impressed because at last he could play loudly. He played with such volume that I had to ask him to turn it down as it was

> drowning all of us. He was like a child with a new toy.
>
> Of course, to be fair, he didn't know how to handle it. We'd heard Charlie Christian and (he) was a master of the electric guitar." Grappelli went on to say that, "Django was born to play acoustic guitar and the richness of Django was in his chords and he could never achieve the same dynamic effect that he could from his acoustic guitar. He never succeeded to play electric and in my opinion he never was a good electric guitarist."

Personally, I don't set much store by Stephane's account of the dates. Not only have we seen evidence that Django had experimented with the electric instrument a year or so earlier but I can find no record of them having played the Hackney Empire since the 1930s. I'm not alone in doubting his powers of accurate recollection - Stephane has been described elsewhere as being, "particularly flexible with dates and memories."

As regards Stephane's opinion of Django's electric playing style, I'm pretty sure it was simply a case of sour grapes. Although they obviously respected each other and worked well together, I'm not sure they were ever the closest of friends and after not seeing each other during the war years, things were never the same as they had been before. I believe Django wanted to move on. He could have re-united with Stephane and the others from the `Hot Club *de France' era but chose not to.*

In his last few years, Django assembled outfits featuring a wide range of other musicians, replacing the violinist with other instrumentalists including clarinetists, sax players and pianists. He also played electric guitar almost exclusively.

~~~~~~~~
~~~~~~~~

2 What they say about the guitar

I love to hear what guitarists and other musicians have to say about the instrument and I think that like me, you might be a little surprised at some of the names that crop up here.

Who'd have thought for instance that Niccolo Paganini, the most celebrated violin virtuoso of his time, and still regarded today as one of the pillars of modern violin technique, was also an accomplished guitar player who said of his instrument:

> "I love the guitar for its harmony; it is my constant companion on all my travels."
>
> *Niccolo Paganini*
>
> "The violin is my mistress, but the guitar is my master."
>
> *Niccolo Paganini*

Or that Frederic Chopin, known chiefly for more than two-hundred piano compositions, said of the guitar:

> "There is only one thing more beautiful than one guitar - two guitars."
>
> *Frederic Chopin*

"The (guitar is the) instrument most complete and richest in its harmonic and polyphonic possibilities."

Manuel de Falla

"The guitar is a wonderful instrument which is understood by few."

Franz Schubert

"I don't play the guitar, I play with the guitar. No guitar can be perfectly tuned."

Jacques Vincenti

"The guitar is the easiest instrument to play, and the hardest to play well."

Andre Segovia

"Discovering the guitar is like finding a new continent that exists within your fingertips."

Will Hodgkinson (in "Guitar Man")

"The guitar's most special quality is its ability to shape the dying away of a sound into silence."

John Williams

"Of all the instruments, the guitar produced the most positive responses in the persons involved in this investigation".

Mary Lou Fitzgerald-Cloutier (from `The Effects of Different Musical Instruments Used for Accompaniment on Participation for Persons Diagnosed with Probable Alzheimer's Disease')

"A good player can make any guitar sound good"

Michael Bloomfield

"I wish they'd had electric guitars in cotton fields back in the good old days. A whole lot of things would've been straightened out."

Jimi Hendrix

"The guitar is just a wonderful instrument. It's everything: a bartender, a psychiatrist, a housewife. It's everything, but it's elusive."

Les Paul

"Besides being a guitar player, I'm a big fan of the guitar. I love that damn instrument."

Steve Vai (from Guitar Player, May 1995)

"I would not even grace my firegrate with one of those."

Kent Armstrong on Mexican Fenders (contributed by Nic Lucas)

“First guitars tend to be like first loves: ill-chosen, unsuitable, short-lived and (yet) unforgettable.”

Tim Brookes (in “Guitar: An American Life”)

“One cannot become a guitarist if he has not bathed in the fountain of culture.”

Agustin Barrios Mangore

“The guitar is a meditative tool to touch God and find love within yourself. Look for the perfect truth in the pieces you play. Playing a piece too fast is betraying the truth to ourselves and the universe, producing more garbage sounds and littering the universe. Nerves never attack a person in love.”

Pepe Romero, Jul 5, 1998

"The guitar is your first wings. It's assigned and designed to unfold your vision and imagination."

Carlos Santana

“This is the fascination of this instrument. It makes people happy.”

Sandra Papachristos

Claude Debussy about the guitar: "The guitar is an expressive harpsichord." It was after he listened to my playing that the great master was inspired to say this sentence. Many people are not aware of that, but I want to point it out with the legitimate pride of an artist."

Miguel Llobet

"The guitar, by its very nature, the nature of its sound, by the soft nuance of its powerful and ancient voice, by the magic of the tone, goes directly to the part of oneself where love is felt. When I hear the sound of the guitar, it goes to some part inside of me that opens the door that holds feelings of love and everything that is beautiful which lives inside of me."

Pepe Romero

"I don't know, with a piano, in a sense you're stuck with the sound of the piano so you can only do things which use that sound. Anyway, I never cease to be amazed by what you can say with the guitar."

John Williams

"I don't have any limits, or feel any limits in the guitar. I consider it a small orchestra, and almost perfect. People discover that the guitar has a very small sound. This could be a defect or a quality. I consider it a quality for intimacy. The guitar has all the colors, and the polyphony, and many, many things - except powerful sound. You can communicate completely. And there's a magic tone that you can get out of the guitar. In fact, the guitar is one of the few minor instruments, like harpsichord and recorder, which not only remains but develops and grows. The polyphony which has evolved with the guitar helps to include a modern language, along with the heritage form the Renaissance up to now. So we are millionaires in terms of repertoire, color and expressiveness! Other instruments have magic but not history. We have all!"

Leo Brower

"La guitarra es como una dama.. donde no cabe la escusa de mírame y no me toques" Gaspar Sanz, 1640 (The guitar is like a lady... there's no room for the excuse of "look at me, but don't touch me") ("Tocar" means in Spanish two things: touch or play. So "play the guitar" is "Tocar la guitarra", and "touch a woman" is "Tocar la mujer")

“Be a musician first and a guitarist second.”

Juan Mercadol

"The guitar is my favorite instrument. I like piano and violin too but guitar is something else."

Arash Alavi

"The guitar has a kind of grit and excitement possessed by nothing else."

Brian May

“One day you pick up the guitar and you feel like a great master, and the next day you feel like a fool. It’s because we’re different every day, but the guitar is always the same. Beautiful.”

Tommy Emmanuel (contributor Nuno Barreto)

"The only reason we play the guitar is that we can have different sounds. What are the other reasons to the play the guitar? Not for volume, not for polyphony (more than flute but less than piano), not for range of sound, but for the color, the quality of the sound."

Luigi Biscaldi

"The turning point in the history of western civilization was reached with the invention of the electric guitar."

Lene Sinclair

“If you really love guitar, you’re going to spend every waking hour stroking the thing.”

Frank Zappa

"Just because a guitar is old doesn't make it good... I've seen guitars that were old but weren't as good as the reissue. For me, it's not the age that makes it happen, it's the quality of the instrument."

Jorma Kaukonen

"There are two means of refuge from the miseries of life - guitars and cats."

Albert Schweitzer (1875-1965)

"A guitar has moonlight in it."

James M. Cain"

The harmonious efforts which our guitarists produce unconsciously represent one of the marvels of natural art."

Manuel de Falla

My guitar, I sing of thee

'Tis with thee that I decoy

And ensnare enchantingly the ladies I enjoy.

Pierre de Ronsard

"The only time you saw a guitar was in the hands of a cowboy in a western film singing 'Home on the Range'."

Bert Weedon commenting on how rare it was to see a guitar when he was a young man.

~~~~~~~~

And I also love to hear what guitarists have to say about their own and other instruments.

"Oh yeah, I mean, it wasn't a very good guitar, most good guitars have got truss rods in the necks that you can adjust or that'll keep them in shape, you know keep them straight. This one just, well it turned into a bow and arrow after a couple of months."

Eric Clapton (talking about one of his early guitars)

"My heart and soul are in the Stratocaster."

Adrian Belew
~~~~~~~~

The Strat covers the complete spectrum of human emotion .. the tremolo enables you to do anything - you can hit any note known to mankind."

Jeff Beck

"I figured out how to get the guitar to rumble. I put it on the middle pickup, turn the tone knob down, grab it by the wang bar, and just shake it on the floor. A Stratocaster is pretty tough. I wouldn't recommend that anybody do that with their ES-335."

Stevie Ray Vaughan

"I mainly use Stratocasters. I like a lot of different kinds of guitars, but for what I do, it seems that a Stratocaster is the most versatile. I can pretty much get any sound out of it, and I use stock pickups."

Stevie Ray Vaughan

"There's something about the Strat's shape that is at once masculine and feminine."

Bonnie Raitt

"A Strat was a thing of wonder. When I was fourteen or fifteen, the Shadows were a big influence, and they had the first Strats that came to England. I like to play all kinds of guitars, but I wasn't getting the sound I really wanted until I got a Stratocaster."

Mark Knopfler

"When I was in Nashville, Tennessee in 1970 with Derek and the Dominoes, I went into this shop and they had a rack of Strats and Teles - all going for $100.00 each. I bought a handful and made Blackie out of the body from one, the neck from another, and so on."

Eric Clapton

"The only thing I ever really wanted was a Strat. I started playing guitar after seeing Jimi Hendrix on TV the day he died. Then I got Deep Purples' Fireball album which was also a big influence. I have a collection of more than 200 of them that includes Strats from every year since March 1954 - the first month the Strat was made."

Yngwie Malmsteen

“The Telecaster has two sounds - a good one and a bad one.”

Jimi Hendrix

“All of the great sounds that James Burton and Jimmy Bryant were getting came out of Telecasters."

Albert Lee

"I was doing someone's hair the day I first saw my guitar. A guy was walking down the street with it, and I knew that guitar was mine (a 1953 weathered Fender Telecaster). I said, "I'll get you the most beautiful guitar you've ever seen and I'll trade you straight across". I found him a purple Telecaster and said, "Here's your guitar." That was it, it was like he knew that guitar belonged to me."

Roy Buchanan

"When I take my Les Paul onstage, it's reliable. An SG could be different from night to night, but a

Les Paul is so solid and reliable that you can trust it every night."

Peter Svensson (The Cardigans)

"I got the Les Paul. It felt awfully cold, so about six months later I traded it for the ES-175."

Jim Hall

"Jimmy Page bought a Les Paul because he liked mine, but it was stolen, so he bought a Standard everybody raved about. That's what he's famous for, but his first Les Paul was a Custom like mine. I can remember he played a Gretsch before that."

Albert Lee

"I have enough trouble dealing with the intricacies of the 6-string."

Jim Hall (On 7-string guitars)

"The instrument keeps me humble. Sometimes I pick it up and it seems to say, "No, you can't play today." I keep at it anyway, though."

Jim Hall

“The guitar is still a mystery to me.”

Jim Hall

"I've always stuck with the same basic kind of Gibson, like the model I play now, an ES-175. It's the only kind of electric I've ever played when I had a choice. I've had this one since 1963.

Back in my Synanon days, I didn't have a guitar of my own. All I had was a solid body rock and roll guitar that belonged to Synanon. I was playing a gig at a local club with it when this guy named Mike Peak came in and saw me playing jazz with a rock guitar. A few months later, on my birthday, I came home and there was this brand new ES-175 that he had bought for me. He was in the construction business and played a little guitar himself and just felt that I should have the proper kind of instrument. It's the only electric I've used since then."

Joe Pass (from Jazz Guitar)

"By then I was getting a little work, doing some playing and getting paid for it, not very much, but enough for me to feel justified in buying a real instrument. I bought a Gretsch with a De-Armond pickup on it and a second-hand Gibson amplifier. It looked like the one Charlie Christian used. I guess it was the same, although there were several models coming out at that time - this would be in 1939."

Tal Farlow (from Jazz Guitar)

And despite being closely identified with particular models, some players claim it doesn't matter much to them what they play.

"Every guitarist I would cross paths with would tell me that I should have a flashy guitar, whatever the latest fashion model was, and I used to say, 'Why? Mine works, doesn't it? It's a piece of wood and six strings, and it works."

Angus Young

"I got a standard box. I don't never want nothing special. Then if I drop my box, I can borrow somebody else's."

Wes Montgomery (from Jazz Guitar)

"I didn't want to get attached to one guitar. I didn't want to have an instrument that was irreplaceable."

Robin Trower

"I wanted a Gibson type sound, but with a Strat vibrato. I bought a body from Charvel for $50.00, a neck for $80.00, slapped it together, put an old Gibson PAF in it and painted it with the stripes."

Eddie Van Halen

"One important thing to me is that Barney Kessel is the first guitarist I ever saw who said, 'You need eight guitars to be a session guitarist'. I only had about four at the time. And when I saw his 'eight guitars' quote I kinda read what he meant. Like having a 12-string. Barney put something very influential in my head about the multi-guitar idea when he mentioned eight guitars including 12-

string and mandolin. That well-rounded idea obviously affected me when I went into doing 'Monster Guitars'."

Steve Howe (interviewed in 2003)

"Michael Bloomfield was the antithesis of a collector. He didn't care how old a guitar was; all he wanted was something that sounded good when played it. He cared nothing about the collectability of an instrument. His philosophy was, "A good player can make any guitar sound good". To Michael, a guitar was just a tool."

Nick Gravenites (Electric Flag)

Not many people have ever been lucky enough to get up close and personal with Django's own guitar so I though you might like this little piece from one guy who had a rare opportunity to examine it for himself.

"I then examined his battered guitar. Django told me had had it eight years. It certainly showed signs of wear and little of its original polish remained. The strings were extremely light gauge and when I played a few chords I was amazed at the lowness of the action. The plectrum

Django uses is the usual pear-shaped pick, of medium size, extremely thick and with a heavy bevel.

The case in which Reinhardt carries his guitar is sadly knocked about. The original handle is missing and is replaced by a piece of wire. What covering the case formerly possessed has long disappeared. Django shrugged expressively when he saw me looking at the case. "Cest la guerre," he said. Incidentally, he had not brought any spare strings with him and when one snapped during the `run through', Jack Llewellyn came to the rescue."

Sam Adams of BMG magazine, 1946

~~~~~~~~
~~~~~~~~

LIFE BEFORE LEO

"I wonder if young players today know just how lucky they are to have really good quality instruments available at such low prices - and I do mean incredibly low - I'm talking about perhaps $1/20^{th}$ of the price that they once were.

When they were first available in the UK, a Fender Stratocaster cost the equivalent of about £6,000 today and none of us could afford one. Eric Clapton was playing a Kaye, Jimmy Page and George Harrison had Hofner Futuramas and Jimi Hendrix played a dreadful old Supro.

In the UK at the start of the '60s, only Hank Marvin was able to ditch his first electric instrument (an Antoria that wouldn't stay in tune) for a real Strat, Cliff Richard having made enough money by then to buy him one.

As for me, I bought one of Jim Burns' early creations, a Burns Sonic, for a barely affordable 55 guineas (still nearly £2,000 in today's money).

It wasn't a bad instrument, in fact it was good by the standards of that time, but neither it nor any of the others would come even close to the quality of a £100 guitar today."

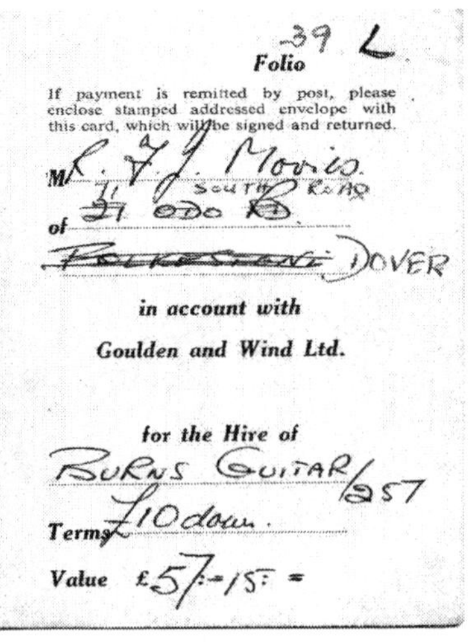

39 L
Folio

If payment is remitted by post, please enclose stamped addressed envelope with this card, which will be signed and returned.

Mr. R. F. J. Morris.

of 71 South Road ~~27 Odo Rd~~

~~Folkestone~~ Dover

in account with

Goulden and Wind Ltd.

for the Hire of

Burns Guitar /257

Terms £10 down.

Value £57-15-

Mick Morris (Interview by Gibson Keddie of `Guitarist' magazine. Published in `Gear' magazine 2009)

~~~~~~~~
~~~~~~~~

3 The funny side of things

In the mid-1960s, Don Adams was a guest on Jimmy Dean's network television show. He mentioned to Jimmy that his wife had given him a guitar for Christmas, and he was really enjoying it. Jimmy was surprised, and asked Don if he'd like to play something. Don said sure, and a stage hand rolled in a Fender Twin and handed Don a Gibson ES-335.

Don spent a few seconds putting on the strap, plugging the guitar into the amp, and setting the controls. Then he spent a few more seconds tuning up. At that point, he put his index finger on the tenth fret on the high E (string) and plucked a solid D note. He then sat back, satisfied, and took his hands off the guitar.

Dean looked puzzled, waited a moment and then asked, "Is that it?" "Yep," replied Adams. Dean still looked puzzled. He said, "Well, it's just that other guitarists seem to move up and down the neck, playing a lot more notes."

"Well, yeah," said Adams, "they're looking for it. I found it."

~~~~~~~
~~~~~~~

“Every once in awhile I’ll call up Eddie (Van Halen) and ask, “Found that fourth chord yet?”

Billy Gibbons

"Someone told me I should be proud tonight ..... but I'm not, because they kicked me out. ... they did ..... **** them!"

Jeff Beck (addressing his former band-mates when The Yardbirds were inducted into the Rock n Roll Hall of Fame)

In a Rolling Stone feature they were jointly interviewing Jeff Beck and Eric Clapton. Eric was asked if there was anything Jeff does that he can't (I'm paraphrasing - don't have the issue in front of me). Eric replies, "that stuff Jeff does with his right hand - it's like multitasking or something".

When they asked Jeff if there's anything Eric does that he can't do, he replies, "No".

Both break out laughing. I love that.

Anonymous contributor

The origin of one of my favourite anecdotes unfortunately seems to have gone AWOL. It's something I read some years ago but have been unable to track down again recently. That won't stop me telling it to you but if I've got anything wrong or if anyone can identify the source I'd be grateful if you'd let me know.

It concerns a young Robbie Robertson who had not long since joined the Hawks, Ronnie Hawkins band. Robbie was in the studio to lay down a guitar solo. He'd played it several times already but Ronnie Hawkins repeatedly asked him to play it again. Being new to studio work, Robbie didn't like to question Ronnie's judgment but after a while felt sure his playing was getting worse rather than better.

> "What's actually the problem Ronnie", said Robbie.
>
> "String noise man, too much string noise", replied Ronnie.
>
> Plucking up his courage, Robbie said, "The thing is Ronnie, everybody gets *some* string noise you know. I mean, like even Andres Segovia gets *some* string noise."
>
> Without breaking his stride, Ronnie replied, "Yeah, I heard about that. And that's why that f****r's never gonna be in my band."

"Rod (Stewart) and I have a love/hate relationship - he loves me and I hate him!"

Jeff Beck

“My first wife said, 'It's either that guitar or me' you know - and I give you three guesses which one went.”

Jeff Beck

“Link Wray and Gene Vincent.... two of the greatest unknowns of rock ‘n’ roll.”

John Lennon

“God has a way of telling you when to change your strings.”

Dave van Ronk

“If something is too hard to do, then it’s not worth doing. You just stick that guitar in the closet next to your shortwave radio, your karate outfit and your unicycle and we’ll go inside and watch TV.”

Homer Simpson

Interviewer - "Keith Richards was quoted as saying that you (Taj Mahal) are the whitest blues guitarist/musician he's ever heard."

Taj Mahal - "Well, he would know wouldn't he?"

During a Willie Nelson interview the interviewer asked Willie if he had given any thought to retiring. Willie responded, "All I do is play guitar and golf. Which one should I give up?"

"By the way, Barney Kessel can kiss my `lack of standard method' ass. My palm rests on the bridge, and my hapless pinky and ring finger just pass time hanging out on or around the pickguard. I can't tell them where to spend their free time. And yes, I have been drinking."

Bob Wire (guitarist)

"If a man knows how many guitars he's got, then he hasn't got enough."

(Ralph McTell in concert Birmingham Town Hall June 2009)

Barney Kessel appeared in the 1944 Academy Award nominated Warner Brothers short feature, 'Jammin' The Blues'. He was the only white musician in an otherwise all black band that included one of his two heroes, tenor sax guru Lester 'Pres' (the President) Young. (Kessel's other hero was black electric guitar pioneer, Charlie Christian).

But producer Jack Warner was concerned about losing money in the South from likely boycotting because of Kessel's presence with the otherwise all black musicians, so he had the cameraman shoot Kessel from a distance and in the shadows.

When that didn't work, Warner told his make-up department to darken Kessel's face and hands. After several attempts, Barney ended up darker than Lester Young who was a light-skinned Negro. When Lester saw him he burst out laughing and said they'd better `start putting some of that stuff' on him!

~~~~~~~

Barney Kessel performed on all the mid-period Beach Boys hits such as 'I Get Around', 'California Girls' and 'Dance, Dance, Dance', including the later Brian Wilson productions such as 'Pet Sounds', 'Good Vibrations' and 'Smile'.

Top session bassist, Carol Kaye, remembers an incident during one of the many 'Pet Sounds' recording sessions.
~~~~~~~

"Brian Wilson was so proud of a multi-voice part of about 12 tracks or so he had single-handedly cut, he played it for us and we were all amazed. Barney Kessel couldn't get over it, and this from a famous jazz man. Barney tuned to Brian and said, 'Brian, I take back everything I ever thought about you!'"

From a Spectropop article by Harvey Kubernik with kind permission of David Kessel

~~~~~~~~

(David) Letterman asked Duane Eddy what he felt his greatest contribution to rock and roll was. Duane said, "Probably, not singing."

~~~~~~~~

> "We didn't have any instruments, so I had to use my guitar."
>
> *Mother Maybelle Carter*

~~~~~~~~

Playing on Frank Sinatra's recording `Strangers In The Night', Glen Campbell recalls that he was so dumbstruck by being in the presence of the master that he couldn't stop staring at him.

> "Frank asked the producer Jimmy Bowen, 'Who's the fag on guitar over there?'"

~~~~~~~~

"It took me twenty years to learn I couldn't tune too well. And by that time I was too rich to care."

Chet Atkins

Chet Atkins was in a Nashville studio warming up for a session with his Gretsch. A young technician came into the studio and stood watching open-mouthed until Chet finished.

> "Gee, Mr Atkins, that guitar sure sounds fabulous!"

Chet placed the guitar on its stand, smiled at the tech and said,

> "Well, son, how does it sound now?"

~~~~~~~~

During an interview, Ravi Shankar was asked "How is it that you are so more technically advanced than other players?" Shankar replied matter-of-factly, "Well, it's my third lifetime playing the instrument."
~~~~~~~~

"Yes, we three were so happy, my wife, my guitar and me!"

Big Bill Broonzy

Ted Nugent: (on plugging into Eddie Van Halen's setup at a big venue) "Hey, that doesn't sound like you". *Eddie:* "Well who the f*** did you expect it to sound like?"

\~~~~~~~~

Roger Miller when asked why he didn't play all that fancy, complicated stuff way up the neck like all the other guitar players do. Without missing a beat Roger says, "All the money's right down here", and points to the first three frets.

\~~~~~~~~

Big Jim Sullivan was once with Chas and Dave when he commented on a record he'd heard.

"If I could only play like that", he said.

"That *is* you, you pillock," said Chas.

"Never having thought of writing for the guitar, I asked Julian Bream for a chart which would explain what the guitar could do. I managed to write some rather pretty pieces for him, except that the first six notes of the first piece all need to be played on open strings. So when he begins to play the audience will probably think he's tuning the bloody thing up!"

William Walton

~~~~~

"A funny thing happened with Django. He was staying at the Hudson Hotel in Manhattan, and I would go up in the afternoon and we'd mess around together, or maybe I'd take him round the city. At this time Les Paul was at the Paramount Theatre so Django and I went down there to visit him in the afternoon. After that, Django invited me to join him at this club where he was working, the Cafe Society, up town and a real hoity-toity place. I didn't even have on a tie and he hadn't shaved, and I didn't want to go in but he insisted I had to be his guest for dinner. So we go into this restaurant and the place was full of people in dinner clothes
~~~~~

and looking immaculate. They put us at a table way over in the corner - I guess to get us out of the way. So we sat there and all of a sudden Django picked up his knife and started banging on the table. People started looking around because by now dishes were falling off the table, and waiters ran over to try to quieten him down. They spoke French, so finally we found out the reason for the commotion: he was insulted because all the other tables had a little glass vase with a flower in it and our table didn't. And he's just tore up the joint because that was an insult!"

From a feature on Johnny Smith, "Guitar" magazine, August 1976

~~~~~

"I was talking to Duke Ellington in Denver, and I asked him what happened to Django. He said Django went back to Paris, because somebody at the William Morris Agency had beat him playing billiards, and he got mad and left. I think Django considered himself to be a great billiards player and he couldn't stand getting beaten like that."

Chet Atkins (who met Django during his visit to the USA)
~~~~~

For me, the funniest stories about Django are those told by Stephane Grapelli from their years of working together. Here are a few.

> "I don't mind him being a gypsy, you know, but sometimes he don't wash too often. For instance, his feet!"

~~~~~~~~

When Stephane and Django first came to England, they were topping the bill at the London Palladium. On their way to the theatre, Django suddenly pointed up to the sky and said, "It's just like the moon we have in Paris." Stephane had a very difficult time persuading him that it was the same moon.

~~~~~~~~

Something else that Django couldn't understand was the working of the beautiful car he had just bought. About twenty minutes outside of Paris, the car ran out of petrol so Django simply got out, closed the door and caught the next bus. When he arrived at the gig, Stephane enquired as to where his new car was. Django explained that it would no longer go, and he had left it twenty miles away. As far as he was concerned, the fact that it had run out of petrol meant that the car was finished, and he never went back to the spot to recover it.

~~~~~~~~
~~~~~~~~

"I shall never forget the first day Django put on evening dress - with bright red socks. It took me some time to explain, without injuring his feelings, that red socks were not the right thing. Django insisted that he liked it that way, because red looked so good with black."

∼∼∼∼∼∼∼

But I do have one little Django story of my own.

On 10th March 1972, I was at a concert given by the French pianist Jacques Loussier and his trio. I had read that Jacque's bassist, Pierre Michelot had played and recorded with Django and I was lucky enough to get to meet him briefly after the show.

I knew that by the time they had played together, Django was playing electric guitar almost exclusively so I asked Pierre what it was like.

He replied that, " ... he often played very loud .... too loud ..... like your Jimi Hendrix!"

∼∼∼∼∼∼∼

4 Guitarists on themselves

“I don’t know shit from shinola. Maybe that’s why I’m so original.”

Ace Frehley

"I don't see myself as such an important guitarist."

Ritchie Blackmore

"I don't put myself on Jeff Beck's level, but I can relate to him when he says he'd rather be working on his car collection than playing the guitar."

Ritchie Blackmore

“The electric guitar was vital in helping what I’ve achieved. Where would I be without it? Playing awfully quietly, for a start.”

Keith Richards

"When I die they will say I played like shit but it sure sounded good."

Hound Dog Taylor

"My voice is my improvisational instrument, the melody instrument. The guitar is harmonic structure. I'm not a good enough guitarist to improvise on it."

Paul Simon

"There was this big skiffle craze happening for a while in England ... everybody was in a skiffle group... All you needed was an acoustic guitar, a washboard with thimbles for percussion, and a tea-chest - you know, the ones they used to ship tea from India - and you just put a broom handle on it and a bit of string, and you had a bass... you only needed two chords; jing-jinga-jing jing-jinga-jing jing-jinga-jing jing-jinga-jing. And I think that's basically where I've always been at. I'm just a skiffler, you know. Now I do posh skiffle, that's all it is."

George Harrison

"I'm only myself when I have a guitar in my hands."

George Harrison

"I think I could walk into any music shop anywhere and with a guitar off the rack, a couple of basic pedals and an amp I could sound just like me. There's no devices, customized or otherwise, that give me my sound."

Dave Gilmour

"I don't even think whether I play the blues or not, I just play whatever feels right at the moment. I also will use any gadget or device that I find that helps me achieve the sort of sound on the guitar that I want to get."

Dave Gilmour

"Years from now, after I'm gone, someone will listen to what I've done and know I was here. They may not know or care who I was, but they'll hear my guitars speaking for me."

Chet Atkins

“What I'm trying to do is make impressions. I think of myself as a colourist, adding different colours and shades by using different techniques and touching the guitar in different ways. I'd like to play sounds you can see if you've got your eyes closed.”

Lenny Breau

“I’ve been imitated so well I’ve heard people copy my mistakes.”

Jimi Hendrix

“I’m not good enough to be playin’ much acoustic guitar onstage. Man, you gotta get it so right. I mean, the tones, the feel, the sound. Plus, acoustic blues guitar is just that much harder on the fingers. I really appreciate when someone can blow me away with live acoustic blues.”

Johnny Winter

"I wanted to create music that was so different that my mother could tell me from anyone else."

Les Paul

“The blues - it's kind of like a religion, really.”

Peter Green

“When all the original blues guys are gone, you start to realize that someone has to tend to the tradition. I recognize that I have some responsibility to keep the music alive, and it's a pretty honorable position to be in.”

Eric Clapton

“I just wonder where I was when the talent was being given out, like George Benson, Kenny Burrell, Eric Clapton, oh there's many more! I wouldn't want to be like them, you understand, but I'd like to be equal, if you will.”

B.B. King

"If you pruned the tree of jazz guitar, Freddie Green would be the only person left."

Jim Hall

"We were all real excited about this thing, The next morning I called Scotty Moore over at Sun and I said: 'We got a hot one, can you make me a dub on it?' So I ran over and he says, 'Man, that's funky!' Then I took the dub over to Reuben Washington at WLOK and he just threw it on live, played it four times in a row. And I'm tellin' you, the phones lit up."

Steve Cropper

~~~~~~~~
~~~~~~~~

5 Guitarists on other guitarists

For me at least, there were a few surprises in store when I proof read this section. Although as I've already acknowledged, the material included doesn't, and probably couldn't, attempt to be all inclusive, there are nevertheless some unexpected omissions.

Equally surprising to me though are some of the names that crop up time and time again. Some of them - Barney Kessel, Jimi Hendrix, Jeff Beck, Django Reinhardt or Eric Clapton appear so often that they could easily fill whole chapters on their own. But whilst I'm not surprised at that, who'd have expected the name of the relatively little-known Lenny Breau to turn up so many times?

~~~~~~~~

"After I saw Jimi play, I just went home and wondered what the f*** I was going to do with my life."

Jeff Beck
~~~~~~~~

On seeing Jeff Beck's face coming out of the Marquee as he was going in to see Jimi Hendrix's first UK show, Pete Townsend said to Beck, “Is he that bad?” to which Beck replied, 'No, he's that good!'

(contributed by Jonathan Sketcher)

"I couldn't believe how good Jimi Hendrix was. It was a really difficult thing for me to deal with, but I just had to surrender and say, 'This is fantastic. I knew immediately that this guy was the real thing and when he played it was like a rough sketch of what he was going to become. This guy was our generation, and he wasn't in a suit.. he played a Howlin' Wolf song ‘Killing Floor’, and then we (The Cream) had to carry on the set. It was pretty hard to follow.”

Eric Clapton

"I really thought I was pretty good before I saw Hendrix, and then I thought, Yeah, not so good."

Brian May

"I started out playing guitar because Jimi Hendrix was my hero, so my roots were really based on Jimi Hendrix and his style of playing."

Joe Satriani

"You watch Jimi Hendrix literally reinvent the instrument.

He was playing from somewhere else. He was really a kind of hybrid, and I can't even begin to imagine where he came from."

Steve Vai

"Jimi Hendrix could play better than our best guys and he did it while he was dancing while being completely outrageous."

David Crosby

"Jimi Hendrix was the most exciting guitarist I've ever heard."

Brian Jones

"Everyone was using tiny brushes and doing watercolors, while Jimi Hendrix was painting galactic scenes in Cinemascope. We are working in a field of mystical resonance, sound and vibration. That's what makes people cry, laugh and feel their hair stand up."

Carlos Santana

"The music of Hendrix wakes people up to their possibilities. It's more than just dreaming about being a guitar hero."

Carlos Santana

"I did several shows with Jimi Hendrix, that's when I got to know him better, I knew of him, I met him (when he was playing) with Little Richard... and he was kind of quiet, shy, he didn't open up too much, but there were questions as we all ask each other. You know, "how do you do this" and, "why do you do that..." We had very small discussions on things like that. And he was very polite, I thought (he was) a very nice guy."

B.B. King

When Jimi Hendrix played New Years Eve with "Band of Gypsys", he did two shows. The first show, he did all his tricks .. behind the back, with his tongue, humping his axe, etc. The place went nuts. When he came off, he asked Bill Graham, the show's producer, what'd he think? Graham replied, "You did everything but play guitar, Jimi".

"Kessel is as lyrical a guitarist as we have in jazz... a rhythmic natural who can out swing any man in the house."

Jazz Critic, Leonard Feather

"Kessel is a player who is never just standing still at one level."

Wes Montgomery

"Those who have heard my music can sense that I learned a lot from Barney."

Tal Farlow

"Barney Kessel is definitely the best guitar player in this world, or any other world."

George Harrison

"Barney Kessel is a unique guitarist. He swings like every member of the rhythm section wishes he could. He is a true artist."

Andre Previn

"Barney Kessel has become the American jazz icon. He reached the same status as Louis Armstrong."

Mundell Lowe

"I'd listen to Barney Kessel records and my jaw would drop. I was awe-struck by the nature of his ad libs. I followed Barney Kessel's musical stories like a kid following a fairy tale."

B.B. King

"Kessel is #1. His style of guitar is copied so much, but never equalled. Barney Kessel is the greatest guitarist in the universe."

Phil Spector

"Barney Kessel is incredible. He's just amazing. Nobody can play guitar like that. What else can you say?"

John Lennon

"Barney Kessel was a very special man, a good man and a great, great, legendary talent."

Carol Kaye

"When I was on the road with Bob Wills, the Texas Playboys and Tommy and Glynn Duncan, often times Barney would come to the country dance halls to visit. His very presence inspired us to play better."

Jimmy Wyble

"Kessel is transcendental in his artistry."

Henry Mancini

"Barney Kessel nailed me to the cross, twelve ways to Sunday."

Oscar Peterson

"Barney Kessel is the Sir Laurence Olivier of the guitar."

Mickey Rooney

"Barney Kessel was the first American jazz guitarist I ever related to. I started playing when I was 12 in 1959 and I reckon about two years after that I was aware of Barney Kessel. I guess the Kessel album that was most important to me and still is, is 'The Poll Winners' with Shelly Manne and Ray Brown. 'Volume 1', a blue cover, on the Contemporary label. I bought it and most of Barney's albums in London at Dobell's, the famous jazz shop. It was archetypal, real jazz. I bought all the LP's he made when he was the leader. I also liked him in support roles. I have the whole collection of 'The Poll Winners'. One of the things I liked about Barney was his sound. Compared to other players, he had a very earthy, organic quality to his sound. And his playing was a remarkable mixture of 'single line' and 'chords', ya know, which inspired me to believe that any guitarist who doesn't understand chords won't be able to play much in the single line because they relate so much. Barney had his own great, highly individual approach to jazz guitar. The way he combined the chords and that single line. It was a perfect balance, really."

Steve Howe (interviewed in October 2003)

Barney Kessel was 'Mr. Guitar,' the foremost jazz guitarist of his generation. He had an amazing imagination, his solos were incredible, he swung his tail off, he was a heck of an arranger and could out-read anybody."

Larry Coryell (from Jazz Guitar)

"Every time I listen to Jeff Beck, my whole view of guitar changes radically. He's way, way out, doing things you never expect."

Brian May

"I would say seeing the original Yardbirds with Jeff Beck and Jimmy Page at the old Fillmore was a pretty powerful influence on me."

Ronnie Montrose

"Jeff Beck is my idol. Sometimes he finds notes that I just do not have on my guitar. I can turn on some jazz guitarist and he won't do a thing for me if he's not playing electrically. But Jeff Beck's great to listen to."

Ritchie Blackmore

"I always use the Jeff Beck model. Jeff is just a genius, and he keeps getting better. If there's anybody in your field you want to aspire to be like, it is a guy who does what he wants to do. Every record at least he comes out with one thing that makes everybodys' jaw drop. I would hope that Jimi Hendrix would have done that, although the odds are against him because he did so much in such a short amount of time."

Joe Satriani

"The Yardbirds actually asked me to join their band twice. They asked me before Eric Clapton had even left the band, because their manager wanted to get more commercial and Eric wanted to get more purist; their manager wanted to force him out. Then they asked me again when Eric finally left. But I was still too nervous about getting ill while on the road, and I wasn't quite sure about the politics with Eric Clapton, because we were friendly. So I recommended Jeff Beck, who I think was amazing as far as pushing the Yardbirds to the next level. His imagination on those Yardbirds albums is incredible."

Jimmy Page

“When God plays guitar he uses Jeff Beck's hands.”

Steve Lukather

"I started off trying to play like Big Bill Broonzy .... and I'm still trying."

John Renbourn (quoted on the sleeve of 'Sweet Child')

"As much of a great guitar player as Jimi (Hendrix) was, Bert Jansch is the same thing for acoustic guitar ... and my favourite."

Neil Young

Martin Carthy recalled that when Bert Jansch descended on London's burgeoning folk-guitar scene from his hometown of Edinburgh, his reputation had already preceded him.

> "People talked about Bert as being a bloke who'd only been playing a few months and had already learned everything his teachers could throw at him."
>
> *Martin Carthy (quoted in Pete Paphides' article in The Guardian, Thursday 6 October 2011)*

"Paul Simon used to follow me around," Bert recalled, "and we would play these little places on the outskirts of London for £5 a gig."

~~~~~~~~

Jimmy Page remembered being, "absolutely obsessed" with Bert Jansch. Talking about that eponymous debut album, the Led Zeppelin man said:

> "It was so far ahead of what everyone else was doing. No one in America could touch that."

~~~~~~~~

To say Bert was blessed with a natural affinity with the guitar is as big an understatement as they come. The Scottish folk singer Archie Fisher said it took him just two lessons to teach Bert everything he knew. It would have only taken one, but on the first lesson they went out and got drunk. When blues duo Sonny Terry and Brownie McGhee came to Edinburgh, Bert cornered McGhee after the show and asked him to play Key to the Highway one more time. By the following morning he had mastered it.

(quoted in Pete Paphides' article in The Guardian, Thursday 6 October 2011)

"Eric Clapton is my dream guitarist. I went to London and performed in Eric Clapton's concert at the Royal Albert Hall. I'll work with him any time he asks me."

Carole King

"I thought Eric Clapton was good. He still is. Not only is he good - he's rock's #1 guitarist, and he plays blues better than most of us."

B.B. King

“I was very influenced by Eric Clapton and Jimi Hendrix, both of whom I had the pleasure of playing with and becoming friends with.”

Mick Taylor

“The blues appealed to me, but so did rock. The early rockabilly guitarists like Cliff Gallup and Scotty Moore were just as important to me as the blues guitarists.”

Jimmy Page

"I would just like to say that Ritchie Blackmore did a bunch of great stuff guitar-wise. I'm happy to play the solo from 'Highway Star'. I always thought it was one of the most exciting guitar solos I'd ever played."

Steve Morse

"Hank (Hank B. Marvin) has such a dangerous tone, which is only safe in the hands of a master.

You can see why he spends so much time tuning up because, when you play the way he plays, you simply cannot make any mistakes. There's no bullshit runs - it's always straight-ahead, simple solos, every one a beauty."

Jeff Beck

"Hank never played a phrase which he could only just stretch to - every note was given its true voice - technical perfection."

Brian May (in `The Story of The Shadows.')

"It started basically because of the Shadows and Hank Marvin. He was really the reason I wanted to be a guitar player."

Peter Frampton

More than four decades later he got Marvin to play on his album, 'Fingerprints' saying, "It was like a dream come true."

Hank Marvin is listed by Frank Zappa as an influence on the first Mothers of Invention album. Canadian guitarists Randy Bachman and Neil

Young have also credited Marvin's guitar work as influential. Carlos Santana's nickname in his formative years was Apache because it was one of the earliest pieces he learned to play.

"My ex-wife was trying to be nice once, so she took me to a concert in Los Angeles. I went with her to Symphony Hall, and the orchestra was playing. When the show started, the spotlight was sharp on this one man, Andres Segovia, and he had sombrero on and his guitar propped up like this and, oh man - he was a master! I really heard it. That one guitar sounded like a whole orchestra to me."

B.B. King

"Andres Segovia literally created the genre of classical guitar, which hadn't existed before around 1910. There was flamenco, which he borrowed from, but he actually arranged the works of Mozart and other classical composers for guitar, something that had never been done before. Segovias' style is not slick or contrived, but it's still very clean and his timing is impeccable ... it's got a feeling of casual elegance, as if he's sitting around the house in Spain with a jug of wine, just playing from the heart.."

Roger McGuinn

"Hearing Andres Segovia in person was quite a revelation. It was a knockout."

Julian Bream

"There is no finer guitarist than Kenny Burrell"

George Benson

"Kenny Burrell is overall the greatest guitarist in the world and he's my favorite."

B.B. King

"Kenny Burrell - that's the sound I'm looking for."

Jimi Hendrix

"Kenny Burrell is a great musician and his music has helped to make me what I am today."

Stevie Wonder

"I've always wanted the sound of Muddy Waters' early records, only louder."

Eric Clapton

“Elmore James only knew one lick, but you had the feeling that he meant it.”

Frank Zappa

"John McLaughlin has given us so many different facets of the guitar. and introduced thousands of us to world music, by blending Indian music with jazz and classical. I'd say he was the best guitarist alive. When the band I had with Rod Stewart broke up, I was left wondering what to do. While the charts were full of stuff like "Chirpy Chirpy Cheep Cheep", I became aware of this underground music scene. And what hit me right between the eyes was John's playing on Miles Davis's, "A Tribute to Jack Johnson". That changed everything.

After that, a new chapter of rock music was formed, with his blistering performances with The Mahavishnu Orchestra and everything else. And John's been at it ever since. He's a hard one to keep up with."

Jeff Beck

Jeff seems to like everybody!

"By far the most astonishing guitar player ever has got to be Django Reinhardt ... Django was quite superhuman, there's nothing normal about him as a person or a player. And you can't forget Gene Vincent's guitarist Cliff Gallup - he was my guiding light through my teenage years. If you want to take a broader view, I think country guitarist Albert Lee is a gas. There's also Paul Burlison, who played with Johnny Burnette. People don't think of Les Paul as a rocker, but as far as I'm concerned he laid down the building blocks of rock and roll. From a jazz perspective there's Charlie Christian, Thumbs Carlyle, Grant Green - they're all fabulous players. You can't forget Buddy Guy, I once saw him throw the guitar up in the air and catch it in the same chord. Eddie Van Halen brought tapping to the forefront and I still think he was one of the tastiest players doing it. George Harrison's got great intonation. Eric Clapton is certainly the ambassador - he's the guy everybody makes reference to - he's the household name for electric guitar, blues and rock and roll. Eric's got so much to offer, in addition to playing so well, he gives the world songs they can identify with."

Jeff Beck

"My favourite version of Black Magic Woman is the Fleetwood Mac version, Peter Green. Beautiful sounding guitar. Peter Green was a great writer. There was a three-year period in the late'60s when the guy could do no wrong. That creative output in such a short period of time yielded classic after classic. He's a real unsung hero."

Joe Bonamassa

"B B King, the master and the only King of the blues shows us all why he was the best ever. He had a heart and compassion that reached beyond show business."

Joe Bonamassa

"One of my favourite and criminally underrated blues players of all time (is) Chris Cain. Chris has influenced me for as long as I owned a guitar. Tone and magic phrasing, killer voice and songs to boot."

Joe Bonamassa

"Joanne (Shaw Taylor) is my good friend. She's a wonderful blues artist from the British tradition and a terrific songwriter. We bonded over our mutual love of classic British blues."

Joe Bonamassa

"There's only one Sabbath guitarist and he is the architect for everything, Tony Iommi".

Zakk Wylde

"Pete Townshend is one of my greatest influences. More than any other guitarist, he taught me how to play rhythm guitar and demonstrated its importance, particularly in a three-piece band."

Alex Lifeson

“We must all own up that without Les Paul, generations of flash little punks like us would be in jail or cleaning toilets.”

Keith Richards

"When Ray Flacke came out, it was like 'What in the heck is this?' ... there's a guy who had that Tele players attitude, and he plugged straight into that amp with a delay, and it was unbelievable the way he would bend those big strings. He was really unique."

Brad Paisley

“Albert Lee and I have become real close friends and he comes out anytime I’m in the L.A. area and he’ll sit in for the whole show! ... we’ve got a habit of doing that ... it’s fun ... I love to make it a guitar thing and the audience doesn’t know any different - they think he’s some new band member they don’t know. They don’t realize Albert’s the reason we all play Teles!”

Brad Paisley

"You think back to Tele players, and James Burton was the one who started it all. He inspired Roy Nichols (guitar for Merle Haggard & the Strangers), Don Rich (guitar for Buck Owens & the Buckaroos), and guys like that to push the envelope and expand on that sound. I really identify with that kind of thinking. Those guys to me are the reason why any of us do this."

Brad Paisley

"Lenny Breau dazzled me with his extraordinary guitar playing. I wish the world had the opportunity to experience his artistry."

George Benson (from Jazz Guitar)

"Lenny Breau played more great stuff at one time than anybody on the planet, with feeling and tone. He was the best that ever lived, bar none."

Danny Gatton

"Lenny Breau was a genius - inspired and really loose. I loved how he used the guitar as an extension of his inner freedom, because, obviously, on the outside there were a lot of trainwrecks going on. But when you listen to him play, you hear what kind of guy he really is"

Steve Vai

"Lenny Breau had the ability to reach into your heart."

Larry Carlton (from Jazz Guitar)

"Lenny Breau is one of the true geniuses of the guitar - a musician's musician. His knowledge of the instrument and music is so vast. But he's such a tasty player too. I think if Chopin had played guitar, he would have sounded like Lenny."

Chet Atkins

"I don't know whether it was his (Charlie Christian's) melodic lines, his sound or his approach, but I hadn't heard anything like that before. He sounded so good and it sounded so easy, so I bought me a guitar and an amplifier and said now I can't do nothing but play. Really, welding was my talent, I think, but I sort of swished it aside."

Wes Montgomery (from Jazz Guitar)

"Charlie Christian was the biggest influence on me. The sheer beauty of his lines, and the way he played them, gave people no choice except to take notice. Nobody else could do that then. He had no competition."

Herb Ellis

It was by listening to Goodman's band, that I began to notice the guitarist Charlie Christian, who was one of the first musicians to play solos in a big band set-up".

Alvin Lee

"Charlie Christians' contributions to the electric guitar are as big as Thomas Edisons' contributions to the world."

Barney Kessel

"When it came time to hire a guitar player I didn't even have to think about it. Mike Bloomfield was the best guitar player I'd ever heard."

Bob Dylan

"He signed his work. You could always tell when it was Herb Ellis playing"

Barney Kessel

"Link Wray, father of the power chord."

James Sullivan (Rolling Stone.com)

"Though rock historians always like to draw a nice, clean line between the distorted electric guitar work that fuels early blues records to the late '60s Hendrix, Clapton, Beck, Page, Townsend mob, with no stops in between, a quick spin of any of the sides Link recorded during his golden decade punches holes in the theory right quick. If a direct line from a black blues musician crankin' up his amp and playing with a ton of violence and aggression can be traced to a young, white guy doing a mutated form of same, the line points straight to Link Wray. No contest. "

Cub Koda

"Link is a quiet man to meet, easy and courteous. His music, though, betrays that deep inside he gets very very mean very often. I remember being made very uneasy the first time I heard "Rumble" , and yet very excited by the guitar sound.

And his voice - he sounds like a cross between Jagger and Van Morrison, even sometimes like Robbie Robertson.

We met him in New York in 1970 while recording "Who's Next".... this later inspired the b-side "Wasp Man", a tune we dedicated to Link Wray."

Pete Townshend

"I always enjoyed hearing Stevie Ray Vaughan and his group play. You could go see him every night and his greatness was readily apparent."

Eric Johnson

"When I heard "Pride and Joy" by Stevie Ray Vaughn on the radio, I just said "Hallelujah". He was just so good and strong and he would not be denied. He single handedly brought guitar and blues oriented music back to the marketplace"

Dickey Betts

"Duane Allman was one of the best there ever was. When you listen to him, you are hearing a truly gifted individual giving his all to the music, and there is nothing better than that. Duane played music the same way that he rode his motorcycle and drove his car - he was a daredevil, just triple Scorpio, God's-on-my-side wide open. That was part of the romance and I loved

Duane. I have nothing but admiration for him."

Dicky Betts

"I'd been talking about Duane Allman because I'd heard him play on Wilson Picketts' recording of "Hey Jude" and kept asking people who he was so Tom Doud took me and all the rest of the Dominoes to see the Allman Brothers play in Coconut Grove and introduced us.

I said "let's hang out - come back to the studio". We just jammed and hung out. I kept him there, kept thinking up ways to keep him in the room. "Key to the Highway", "Nobody Knows You When You're Down and Out" are first or second takes. Then I'd quickly think of something else to keep him there. I knew sooner or later he was going to go back to the Allmans, but I wanted to steal him! I tried, and he actually came on a few gigs, too but then he had to say, almost like a woman, "Well, you know I am actually married to the Allman Brothers Band and I can't stay with you". I was really quite heartbroken! I'd got really used to him, and after that I felt like I had to have another guitar player.

I had Neal Schon come in for a little while, having met him through Carlos Santana, but by that time Derek and the Dominoes were on the way out"

Eric Clapton

"Back in the day in my teens I was listening to Joe Pass and Wes Montgomery a lot; before that I was listening to what I would call now the more 'simple' jazz players (but still very valid), like Barney Kessel or Johnny Smith; I learnt a lot of voicings from Johnny Smith records. Now, I listen to the old blues players. That's what you'd hear in my house if there was music on. It would be Albert Collins or Albert King."

Larry Carlton

“Another guitar player who had a tremendous influence on my life was Howard Roberts. I’d listened to a lot of Tal Farlow, Johnny Smith and Kenny Burrell, and I was certainly into those guys, but I was awestruck at the intensity and fire in Howards’ guitar playing. For me, it became a roadmap.”

Jeff ‘Skunk’ Baxter

“Scotty Moore plays one of the first really amazing riffs in rock history on Heartbreak Hotel with Elvis Presley. It was dangerous, it scared everybody's parents, which was part of the attraction then as it still is now. It totally blindsided me and made me want to get a guitar and do that.”

Roger McGuinn

"When Lonnie Mack came out with the guitar instrumental "Memphis" I thought, Oh God, finally somebody we guitar players can relate to !"

Dicky Betts

“One summer I remember, I got exposed to Chuck Berry and Buddy Holly and Buddy Holly made a very big impression on me. Because of a lot of things, you know, the way he looked and his charisma.”

Eric Clapton

“I remember hearing Sonny Terry and Brownie McGhee, Big Bill Broonzy, Chuck Berry and Bo Diddley and not really knowing anything about the geography or the culture of the music. But for some reason it did something to me. It resonated."

Eric Clapton

"I admire Eddie Van Halen and Steve Lukather, but they might blow me away quite easily if we were to jam together."

Eric Clapton

"Of the whole bunch of guys who play hollow body guitar, I think Herb Ellis has the most drive."

Les Paul'

"Lightnin' Hopkins was something of a fixture on the Houston coffee house scene so we were witness to eccentric blues brilliance close up."

Billy Gibbons

"I put (Allan) Holdsworth up there with Paganini and Liszt. Terrifying."

David Lindley (from `Guitar Player')

"Allan has the touch. Maybe it's those extra long fingers of his. No one can listen to him without being affected by his tone and fluidity. A superb player who is a joy to hear."

Adrian Belew (from `Guitar Player')

"Holdsworth is so damned good that I can't cop anything. I can't understand what he's doing. I've got to do this (does two-hand tapping) whereas he'll do it with one hand."

Eddie Van Halen (from `Guitar Player')

"Allan really changed guitar playing. The legato techniques and 'sheets-of-sound' approach influenced not only jazz guitarists, but also a whole generation of metal players. And aside from all the technical stuff, he's a master jazz guitarist. Check out his version of 'How Deep Is the Ocean.'"

John Scofield (from `Guitar Player')

"Allan's beautiful and unique chord voicings have always had an impact on me. His approach to guitar is one of a kind. He pushes the limits of the boundaries of electric guitar, and his lead phrasing would make Charlie Parker smile. His playing is essential listening for any guitarist, of any style, so they can see that the only limits we have are the ones we put on ourselves."

Eric Johnson (from `Guitar Player')

"Allan wanted to sound like John Coltrane. Problem was he's playing guitar, not saxophone, so he had to figure out a way to get a similar 'sheets of sound' equivalent on guitar. The scales and intervals he chose were also all unusual, and he didn't become just one of the great scalar improvisers overnight. He worked like a dog on Nicolas Slonimsky's Thesaurus of Scales and Melodic Patterns. Then, when he'd run out of notes he'd reach for the whammy bar and send shivers down your spine."

Bill Bruford (from `Guitar Player')

"I've known Allan and his music for 30 years now, and after all this time he still amazes me. His concept is still advancing with his playing, and his technical prowess, which is phenomenal, is in complete harmony with his musical direction."

John McLaughlin (extract from a longer quote in `Guitar Player')

"When I listen to a guitar player I listen for different things. The first is just the level of stimulation I get as a lover of the instrument and the way it sounds to my ears and soul. Besides being emotionally swept away by Allan's use of melodic color, most of the time I am utterly stunned and confused as to how he is playing what I am hearing. His chops and inner ear completely defy my own inner musical eye and reasoning and I'm left in a blissful state of humility and surrender."

Steve Vai (extract from a longer quote in `Guitar Player')

When I first heard him in about 1973, I was amazed by the ambition and direction of his playing. I was edging along a similar path myself but he was far ahead, and so was a source of inspiration and aspiration. I owe quite a lot to Allan as he recommended me for the guitar post in Soft Machine in 1975 when he left to join Tony Williams. Following Allan was one of the toughest things I ever had to do, as any guitar player can imagine. The set was based around the monumental solos that he had been doing, so I had to try to fill those shoes. He has been ahead of the game for over 30 years and is the preeminent guitar soloist of our generation (if not any).

His playing now is completely controlled and mature and his mastery of the elements that he is interested in - harmony, line and tone - is unique and puts him in the very top league of the greatest soloists in guitar history. That's why guitarists should care!

John Etheridge (extract from a longer quote in `Guitar Player')

(Jim Hall) One of the “twenty-five guitarists who shook the world,"

Guitar Player magazine, 1992

"It was just a very elegant thing that he did that affected all of, just about all of the guitar players after him I think."

John Scofield

"For someone who has had such an impact on just the aesthetic of improvised music and guitar, as a total guitar hero, there was such a degree of humility that - it wasn't that he downplayed what he did - he had this sense that it was part of something way bigger."

Julian Lage

“I was a big fan of Jim Hall. I liked his comping style, his accompanying. And that he played, generally, four note chords, the top four strings of the guitar.”

Gary Burton

"When you have Jim Hall, you don't need a pianist."

Art Farmer

"It could be argued that the jazz guitar tree is rooted in four names: Django, Charlie, Wes, and Jim. Virtually every guitarist, from classical to shred, has been touched by the music that flowed from that quartet. The influence of Hall's music moved well outside jazz circles, with followers including esteemed players like Wilco's sonic wizard Nels Cline and Testament's Alex Skolnick. The beauty and grace of his playing expanded beyond swing with a commanding authenticity."

Premier Guitar - tribute to Jim Hall, 2013

~~~~~~~~
~~~~~~~~

THE LOST RECORD

"There's a strange little story behind this recording. I first heard Jim Hall in the early '60's. I'd been at a party with some friends and it was getting late. Most people had gone and just a few of us musos were left.

The guy whose house we were in had recently left the merchant navy. While in New York, he'd come across a vinyl LP by Jim Hall which had caught his attention because of the name. You see, my friend's name was also Jim Hall.

After the party, he played the album to me. I thought it was the most beautiful guitar playing I'd ever heard. One track in particular stood out for me - a beautiful version of `Embraceable You'.

I played it over and over until I'd memorised the tune. I tried to copy the way Jim played it. I recorded the song myself so I wouldn't forget the arrangement. I've played it many times since and always tell people it's the Jim Hall version.

Some years ago, after buying just about every album he'd made, I realised I still didn't have a copy of the recording I'd first heard. I made a real effort to find a copy of the original recording.

I checked every Jim Hall discography I could find. I found that he'd recorded the tune several times over the years with different line-ups, arrangements etc. but none of them were like the arrangement I'd heard all those years ago. The best of the other versions is of Jim playing in a duo with bassist Ron Carter - very good but it's not the same for me.

I even contacted his agent and pleaded with her to ask Jim but I never got a reply. It's not even listed on his own website. So, according to the official record it never existed! Did I dream the whole thing up or what?

Anyway - if you have been - thanks for reading my little story and listening to one of my favourite melodies."

Mick Morris (text of `Embraceable You' video)

"Usually, no one quite knew where Django Reinhardt was going to be, but I met his brother and about an hour later in walks Django with an entourage of friends. He always traveled with a large group - carried his own admirers with him, the most sinister-looking bunch of hoodlums you've ever seen. I walked up and offered to buy him a drink. That seemed to be the right thing to do.

He was the first really brilliant solo guitarist I ever became aware of. I had records of his when I was ten years old. It just blew my mind that anyone could play a guitar like that. Still does."

Charlie Byrd (from Jazz Guitar)

“We played together, but really, I was just listening because I'd heard him on record and I idolised this man from when I was younger. I'd save up my nickels and as soon as a new record came out I'd be right there. I used to play along with his solos and on the old record player they wouldn't last long and I'd wear them out, so I kept having to get new ones of the old ones too. He really made me realise that the guitar was a musical instrument and not just something to scrape on.”

Extracted from the feature on Johnny Smith in the August 1976 issue of "Guitar" magazine.

“Even if I had complete command of the English language, and even if I knew how to be eloquent, I still don't think I could come up with a word, sentence, or phrase that could adequately describe the way I feel about Django Reinhardt's playing. I have never in my lifetime heard another human being perform with such fire and such love and such emotion. He was in my estimation the freest spirit I'll ever hear on the guitar."

Jerry Reed

"Django was one of the most amazing artists of the first half of the 20th Century. He played `impossible' things on his guitar. The recordings that survive clearly indicate that he was years ahead of most of the people he was playing with. Django represents the universality of modern improvised music.

There will never be another Django. His music, his guitar artistry, everything he was as a person, smacked of genius. I'll bet he smiled a lot."

Larry Coryell

"Django was one of my idols. He had a touch that made him Django Reinhardt and nobody else and as far as I'm concerned, one of the greatest in the guitar business. He'd identify himself on his instrument. Today we've got a lot of great guitarists, but most of them don't identify themselves. But with Django, you knew without a doubt who he was the minute he'd start to play. And to me, it

> was sweet music; his guitar seemed to talk, in other words, I heard it. He played music that was sophisticated to me, but a layman like myself could still understand it. I've got more albums on him than on anybody; when I was in France I must have bought fifty records of the Hot Club Of France. I would never have the speed or the technique that Django had, but I love him so much that I'm sure if you listened carefully you could hear a little bit of him in my playing. I just wish everybody could hear him."
>
> *B B King*

Perhaps it's best for Django's old cohort, Stéphane Grappelli, to have the final word. He summed up Django's playing in the 1954 Melody Maker interview.

> "He did more for the guitar than any other man in jazz. His way of playing was unlike anyone else's, and jazz is different because of him. There can be many other fine guitarists, but never can there be another Reinhardt. I am sure of that."

~~~~~~~
~~~~~~~

6 Learning, practicing and playing

MY FIRST GUITAR

I was thirteen when my Dad bought home an old guitar he'd bought from someone he worked with who'd just upgraded. I was over the moon. I knew nothing about the instrument but couldn't wait to get started.

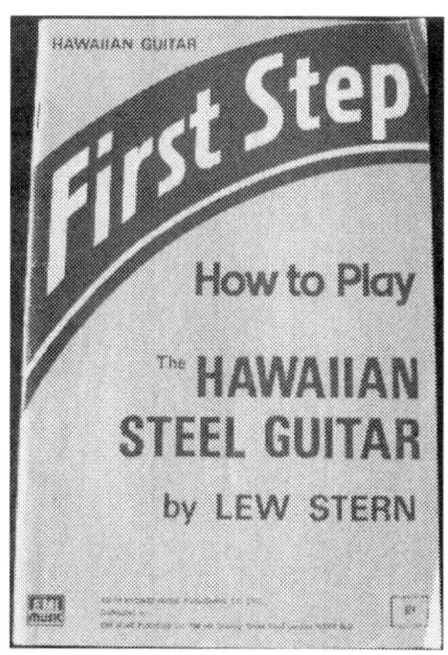

I went to a local music shop to buy a book on how to play the guitar. The manager showed me three tutor books. They were in a series called `The First Step - How to play the .... guitar'. There were three books in the series covering three types of guitar; Spanish, Hawaiian and Plectrum. So, "which one did I have" he asked?

I could only go by appearances. Mine had a flat top, round sound-hole, steel strings and a tailpiece so I opened each book and looked at the pictures just inside the cover.

I ruled out the Plectrum guitar straight away because it was bigger, had an arched top and `f-holes', so mine must be either Spanish or Hawaiian guitar. Neither of them had a tailpiece but both looked otherwise pretty similar to mine.

I noticed that the Spanish guitar book referred to the strings being made of gut or nylon and I knew mine weren't so I bought the Hawaiian guitar book.

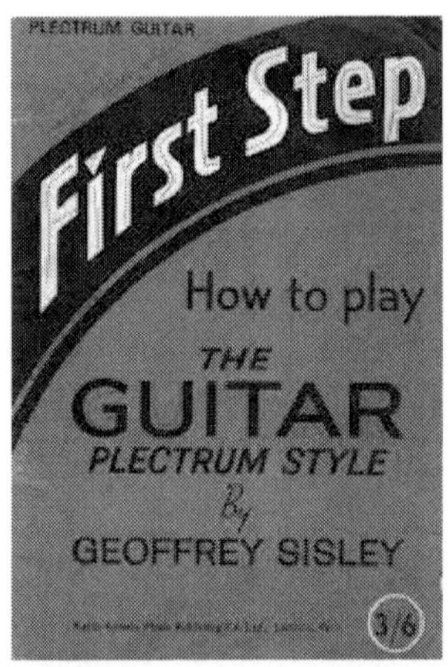

I first suspected something was wrong when I tried to use my pitch pipes to tune it. The book said the guitar should be tuned to E, A, E, A, C#, E but the pipes were tuned E, A, D, G, B, E. Then I looked at the illustration of someone playing it. They had it laid flat across their lap and were producing notes by sliding something up and down the strings. That was definitely not what Lonnie was doing.

I took the book back to the shop and changed it for the Spanish guitar tutor. This time I got it in tune but something was still wrong. Lonnie strummed his guitar, his hand moving down and back again across the strings, playing them all at the same time but the book was telling me to use my thumb and fingers to play separate notes. Again I took the book back to the shop. The manager said, "Well if it isn't either of those it must be a plectrum guitar". He changed the book again and sold me a plectrum.

Eureka! Look out Lonnie, here I come.

(Mick Morris - from `Don't give up the day job')

"George and I went through the Bert Weedon books and learned D and A together."

Paul McCartney

"Bert. Thank you for all those tips on guitar playing that I got from your book, when I was young. I wouldn't have felt the urge to press on without the tips and encouragement that Bert's book 'Play in a Day' gives you. I've never met a player of any consequence that doesn't say the same thing."

Eric Clapton

"Mr. Bert Weedon, Guitar Wizard. This guy is a legend. There are thousands of us so-called guitar heroes who first saw live TV guitar playing by Mr. Bert Weedon. Thank you very much for spreading the guitar and your enthusiasm to all of us, who are very happy to know you."

Brian May

"Bert's book was a great influence on me."

John Miles

"Bert was the first person I ever saw play the electric guitar - he must have had a great influence on me."

Steve Hillage

"Bert was the first guitarist to make any real impression on me. I saw him on a TV show called 'Tuesday Rendezvous' and immediately persuaded my father to buy me my first guitar. In fact if it wasn't for Bert I might never have taken it up in the first place."

Mike Oldfield

"I bought the 'Play in a Day' book and strummed my very first guitar with a Bert Weedon plectrum."

Bill Nelson

"You wait for the Bert Weedon's to come along and show the way."

Sting

"We all started off in our early days through your book 'Play in a Day' - thanks Bert."

John Lennon

"Like everyone else I bought 'Play in a Day', and started off with it."

Pete Townshend

“Learning to play the guitar is a combination of mental and motor skill acquisition. And to develop motor skill, repetition is essential. Whenever musicians have trouble executing a passage, they generally tend to blame themselves for not having enough talent. Actually, all that's wrong is they don't know where their fingers are supposed to go. You should learn the piece in your head before you play it. And when you do play it, play it so slow that there's no possibility of making a mistake."

Howard Roberts

"My style is driven by improvisation - not knowing what will come moment by moment. The other thing is, I like to play like a singer. I hate mindless tinkling guitar. "

Howard Roberts (from Jazz Guitar)

"Whenever you study composition you inevitably encounter Bach right off the bat. You can't get across the room without running into him and the other greats. Analyzing Bach absolutely influenced my jazz playing."

Howard Roberts (from Jazz Guitar)

"I've come up with the theory that the music is within. We don't bring it in; it's already there. We have to figure out how to get it out."

Howard Roberts (from Jazz Guitar)

“Chord substitution isn’t some mysterious religious sect.”

Howard Roberts

“One thing I learned a long time ago was my fretboard in terms of all the scales in all the positions. You have to learn it – there are no two ways about it. I shift between positions so easily now that I really don’t have to think about them much. I would suggest starting your scale education with the major and minor scales and after that, diminished, augmented and whole tone.

Then depending on what kind of music you want to play, the modes should be learned. My theory about this kind of thing is that you should learn it all. Once you've learned it you can play whatever you want to play and I think that your playing will be more advanced and you'll have a better understanding of the instrument."

Al DiMeola

"Forget about every other lesson in the book. You have to be able to tap your foot."

Al Di Meola

"I'd think learning to play the guitar would be very confusing for sighted people."

Doc Watson (who was blind almost from birth)

"I began to learn a lot of chords and rhythms. It was a bit boring at the time but came in very handy later on."

Alvin Lee

“We don’t want any vocalist messing up the music.”

John Scofield

"I actually learned the guitar with the help of a Pete Seeger instructional record when I was thirteen or fourteen."

Dave Gilmour

"I don't have a very disciplined approach to practicing or anything, but I do tend to have a guitar around most of the time, which I strum on most of the day."

Dave Gilmour

“With all these greats (guitar teachers) around here, don’t copy their licks, copy their attitudes.”

Leo Kottke (during a master class)

“I don’t play for the guitarists in the audience. I play for the musicians.”

Frank Gambale

“A lot of people think that if they learn to read music they are gonna lose their feel or their groove or something. It’s the stupidest thing I have ever heard.”

Frank Gambale

"If you get your dream guitar, don't hold back when you play it."

Joe Bonamassa

“I don’t think about what other people expect or anything. I mean, I sit and worry so much about what *I’m* thinking, I’d go nuts if I sat around worrying about other people.”

Allan Holdsworth

"I was my own teacher and pupil, in a comradeship so firm and persevering that the most trying incidents of my life served only to strengthen the union."

Andres Segovia

"When I began, the guitar was enclosed in a vicious circle. There were no composers writing for the guitar, be-cause there were no virtuoso guitarists."

Andres Segovia

"I was my own teacher and pupil, and thanks to the efforts of both, they were not discontented with each other."

Andres Segovia

"When I started to play with my fingernails, it was not just for volume. The most important thing was giving the guitar different colors in its voices."

Andres Segovia

"I've copied more licks from Les Paul than I'd like to admit."

Jeff Beck (when Jeff inducted Les into the Rock and Roll Hall of Fame in 1988)

"You can do a lot more with bare fingers than with a plectrum. You don't get that clunking sound on a heavily amplified guitar. It's also a more personal sound, with more control."

Jeff Beck

"Million-mile-an-hour chops leave me cold. Vocalists don't go didididididi. Why should guitars?"

Jeff Beck

"I'm weird, I really don't play a lot. Most people think that I probably go home to some guitar shop in the sky and practice all day!"

Jeff Beck

"There was mass hysteria in the Chess Recording Studio when I did the "Shapes of Things" solo ... they weren't expecting it, and it was just some weird mist coming from the East out of an amp."

Jeff Beck

"I just didn't know what direction people want, you know music was going down a path, and I couldn't turn on a radio without being disgusted completely. And now it's just gotten to the point where I can't listen to anything, it's trashy. It's just a hundred channels of garbage all over.

And not just here, it's in England as well. It's almost just like a global effort to knock the sense out of you if you're a musician. There's not any little morsel for musicians to latch on to. It's all glossy, lipstick shit. More tits and bare midriffs. Unless you go to a blues club, or some outrageous hip dive somewhere that nobody knows about until the night before, the pickings are slim for inspiration.

I still listen to Django Reinhardt, his catalogue. I'm just catching up with that after several years of not really listening to him properly. You know he's the greatest... it's the fear thing. ... but now I'm getting used to it... He was God. Just amazing."

Jeff Beck

"I'm not saying a guy shouldn't take lessons but if you want to play like the artists, you have to go and get what they're putting on records and take it from there."

Grant Green

"Practicing is not an end in itself. It's purpose is to make sure you are able to play something that you want to play and play it the way you want to play it. You need to think about what that something is because nobody else can tell you."

Mick Morris (from `Play Straight Away')

THE ONLY MACCAFERRI IN TOWN

After I'd been playing for a year or so, my grandad suggested we go to see a guy he knew who played guitar and lived locally. His name was Jack Forth. I thought he was very old - I'd guess he was about the same age as grandad!

In his younger days, Jack had been a well-known local musician and had played regularly with a band who called themselves The Selmas.

Jack had a real pre-war Maccaferri guitar which if it was still around now would be priceless. He let me play it, the only one I've ever played. I found it difficult because the strings were heavy and the action higher than I was used to.

When he played, it reminded me of Django Reinhardt's sound which I'd heard at home on old records.

Jack told me he liked Django very much but that he himself tried to play like his hero, Eddy Lang who at that time I'd never heard of. He asked to see me play something. Not sure what to do, I showed him my latest party trick which was the intro and solo from Eddie Cochran's *Twenty Flight Rock*. Jack very kindly complimented me on my prowess but I think he was just being kind.

When you're as young as I was then, you don't immediately see the connection between players so it was some time before I realised how important Eddie Lang's contribution had been. He may have been the first jazz guitarist. Django was certainly aware of him and so was Charlie Christian and pretty much everything that followed started with them.

(Mick Morris - from `Don't give up the day job')

“It’s very fair to call Eddie Lang the father of jazz guitar. Who did he have to listen to? Eddie didn’t have anyone to copy. He had to develop his individuality by himself. His sound came from inside his head."

George Van Eps

"Eddie Lang first elevated the guitar and made it artistic in jazz."

Barney Kessel

"Eddie Lang was the first and had a very modern technique."

Les Paul

"I taught myself how to play the guitar, so I basically learned by a system of making mistakes."

Richie Sambora

“To be creative and spontaneous, you have to live with imperfection.”

John Abercrombie

"You don't find a style, ... a style finds you."

Keith Richards

"If you don't know the blues, there's no point in picking up the guitar and playing rock and roll or any other form of popular music."

Keith Richards

"Ry, you know some people will use standard tuning while playing slide."

"Really, ... they do? Hmm, I don't think they should do that."

(from a GP interview with Ry Cooder where he is discussing his use of open tunings when playing slide)

"I'm not into that Keith Richard trip of having all those guitars in different tunings. I never liked the Rolling Stones much anyway."

Ritchie Blackmore

"I also generally play slide guitar in standard tuning, which enables me to switch back and forth between using the slide and fretting notes and chords conventionally without having to re-learn the fretboard, as one must do when playing in an open tuning."

Warren Haynes

"My best songs come from making a lot of mistakes and playing a lot of garbage."

Eric Johnson

"I often discover that what sounds great at home sounds hideous in public."

Tuck Andress

"I didn't take lessons, and I don't know my scales. I just find things that work and embellish them."

Lindsey Buckingham

"After a couple of failed attempts, I came up with a weird tuning where I was dropping the G string down a step so that it became a seventh, and it got me to a place where I could play all these figures fairly easily. It was not an easy thing to work out."

Lindsey Buckingham

"All of my style came from listening to records."

Lindsey Buckingham

"Approach your guitar intelligently, and if there are limits, don't deny them. Work within your restrictions. Some things you can do better than others, some things you can't do as well. So accentuate the positive."

Chet Atkins

"Anyone who uses more than three chords is just showing off."

Woodie Guthrie

"Every time you pick up your guitar to play, play as if it's the last time."

Eric Clapton

"When I look for what I'm going to listen to I go backwards. I'm always going the other way you see. Most people are trying to figure out 'how do I get in the fast lane going that way?' I'm going in the other direction. I wanna find the oldest thing to do."

Eric Clapton

"From the beginning, I knew intuitively that if nothing else, music was safe, and that nobody could tell me anything about it. Music didn't need a middleman, whereas all the other things in school needed some kind of explanation".

Eric Clapton

"I never set myself too high a goal. It was always tone and feeling, for me."

Eric Clapton

"I remember when I thought of singing as the bit that went between the guitar playing - something I couldn't wait to get out of the way. Singing was originally like a chore that I didn't really enjoy."

Eric Clapton

“Sight-reading is like playing. It’s a question of doing.”

Johnny Smith

“Don’t be afraid to screw up. One of the key issues to learning is making mistakes. If you’re not making mistakes, you’re probably not having a very good time.”

Robben Ford

“I think of improvising as composing. For me it’s all about playing melodies. When I improvise, there’s not a lot of real thinking going on, per se. It’s more like riding a wave - and I know how to stand on the board.”

Robben Ford

“If you’re not living on the edge, you’re taking up too much space.”

Bob Brozman

“Practice like the Devil.”

Doc Watson

“The greatest teacher is just going out and playing.”

George Benson

“Don’t become so enraptured by certain heroes that your playing is exactly like theirs.”

Jimmy Wyble

"In the past, I tried to be more of a typical session guitarist. I wasn't so concerned with impressing anybody".

Brad Paisley

“From the very beginning when I used to hear those solos on those old records I used to say, now here is an instrument that is capable of spewing forth true obscenity, you know? If ever there’s an obscene noise to be made on an instrument, it’s going to come out of a guitar.

Let’s be realistic about this, the guitar can be the single most blasphemous device on the face of the earth. That’s why I like it. The disgusting stink of a too loud electric guitar: now that’s my idea of good time.”

Frank Zappa (The Guitar Hand Book)

"Well, I get the same sensation listening to Wes Montgomery. You hear Wes when you hear him play, and the same thing with (Allan) Holdsworth. He puts his personality, something about him as a person, into playing, and I don't detect "watch me show off now" - there is none of that syndrome.

That's the thing that is most obnoxious about current guitar, because when people are attempting to play the guitar in a competitive way, in order to do somebody else's style but just do it faster, that's great from an Olympic competition kind of a standpoint, but I don't think it's particularly musical. And since I like music, it would not necessarily excite me to hear someone playing something real fast if it wasn't unique to the individual."

Frank Zappa (on "The '80s Guitar Clone")

"The concept of the rock-guitar solo in the eighties has pretty much been reduced to, Weedly-weedly-wee, make a face, hold your guitar like it's your weenie, point it heavenward, and look like you're really doing something.

Then, you get a big ovation while the the smoke bombs go off, and the motorized lights in your truss twirl around!"

Frank Zappa

I'm more interested in melodic things. I think the biggest challenge when you go to play a solo is trying to invent a melody on the spot."

Frank Zappa

"Don't let your hands dictate what you think you can do. Look at fingerboard charts and imagine your eyes dancing on the notes you want to play, and forget about whether your hands can do it or not. Just try it."

Allan Holdsworth

"I don't play a lot of fancy guitar. - I don't want to play it. The kind of guitar I want to play is mean, mean licks."

John Lee Hooker

"Technique is paramount to the beginner. Only thoughtful, regular, and yes, joyful daily practice will enable the student of the guitar to develop mind muscles and spirit into a concord of execution and expression."

Aaron Shearer

“Sam Phillips always encouraged me to do it my way, to use whatever other influences I wanted, but never to copy. That was a great rare gift he gave me. To believe in myself, right from the start of my recording career. If there hadn’t been a Sam Phillips, I might still be working in a cotton field."

Johnny Cash

“My vocation is more in composition really than anything else - building up harmonies using the guitar, orchestrating the guitar like an army, a guitar army.”

Jimmy Page

"If I pick up a guitar, I don't practice scales. I never have. I come up with something I haven't done before, new approaches to chord sequences, riffs, rhythms, so it becomes composition. It's not like the music I'm doing is just a single thread."

Jimmy Page

"I believe every guitar player inherently has something unique about their playing. They just have to identify what makes them different and develop it."

Jimmy Page

"The blues appealed to me, but so did rock. The early rockabilly guitarists like Cliff Gallup and Scotty Moore were just as important to me as the blues guitarists."

Jimmy Page

“When you play the guitar, you don’t have to say nothing. The girls would say something to you.”

Buddy Guy

"What really cheeses me off is that journalists ask me about the lyrics but they always ask the guys about the music. It's as though they can't take the idea of a woman with a guitar seriously."

Louise Wener

"There are no mistakes, save one - the failure to learn from a mistake."

Robert Fripp

"Fast is only cool if it's melodic and has substance."

Yngwie Malmsteen

"To me a guitar is kind of like a woman. You don't know why you like 'em but you do."

Waylon Jennings

"I don't separate writing songs from poetry and short fiction. In the area where I work in my house, there's a word processor and a guitar."

Steve Earle

"You shouldn't hear the guitar by itself. It should be part of the whole. You only notice the guitar when it's not there."

Freddie Green

“I practice all the scales. Everyone should know lots of scales. Actually, I feel there are only scales. What is a chord, if not the notes of a scale hooked together?”

John McLaughlin

“Shredding, to me, is akin to having a incredibly overblown vocabulary at your disposal and saying very, very little”.

Johnny Marr

"I don't feel part of that group of guitarists (Bernard Butler and Johnny Marr) cos' they all end up going solo and getting boring."

Richard Oakes

"Practicing something fast rarely leads to perfection, but working on accuracy always leads to the ability to play faster."

Jody Fischer (from "Beginning Jazz Guitar")

"For me, the ultimate form of expression is blues, where jazz appeals to me on an intellectual level."

Scott Henderson

"If you play music for no other reason than actually just because you love it, the skills just kinda creep up on you."

Nuno Bettencourt

"It wasn't a class system where I was the better guy and he was the second-rate guy. That was his role and my role was to play the solos. But he took great pride in his technique as a rhythm guitarist."

Wayne Kramer[ii]

"My biggest breakthrough as a player was when I stopped thinking about my playing and just played - stopped apologising for it. I always used to over-think my playing and I'd be consulting the rule-books on stage, whereas now I just play and think if people enjoy it that's great and if people don't that's fine too. The fluidity comes when you turn off the `should I be doing this, should I be doing that' thought process and instead just let it channel out and flow."

Joe Bonamassa

“You can’t think and play. If you think about what you’re playing the playing becomes stilted. You have to just focus on the music I feel. Concentrate on the music, focus on what you’re playing and let the playing come out. Once you start thinking about doing this or doing that, it’s not good. What you are doing is like a language."

Joe Pass

"You have a whole collection of musical ideas and thoughts that you’ve accumulated through your musical history plus all the musical history of the whole world. It's all in your subconscious and you draw upon it when you play."

Joe Pass

"If you hit a wrong note, then make it right by what you play afterwards."

Joe Pass (from Jazz Guitar)

"Guitarists should be able to pick up the guitar and play music on it for an hour, without a rhythm section or anything."

Joe Pass (from Jazz Guitar)

"A guitarist is as good as his/her vibrato."

Francisco Herrera.

"At home I have a guitar in every room, if I break a string I just pick up another guitar."

Kirk Hammett

"I try to practice like a well rounded regiment of things where I can kind of do whatever I wanna do and I also have to practice the actual songs to keep that under my fingers as well."

John Petrucci

"It's hard to describe, because on one hand you want your solo to be spontaneous. On the other hand, I feel a good guitar solo should be somewhat of a composition in itself. So, you sort of toggle back and forth between the concept of trying to initiate flow and composing. I think it's a combination of both."

Jeff 'Skunk' Baxter

"I had struggled with alternate picking for a very long time. I never thought I could do it."

Paul Gilbert

"I'm scared s***less every time I step on stage."

Dave Grohl

"I came from the last couple of years in a generation where we didn't have a computer around so we didn't waste as much time on the internet as we do now so I had large chunks of time which to devote to doing something."

John Mayer

"Every July, August and part of September I escape of the guitar, I escape of Paco de Lucia and I go to Mexico to the Carrabian. I have a little house there where I spend two months listening to music, no playing because I don't bring the guitar with me, fishing and cooking my fish and charging the batteries for new concerts."

Paco De Lucia

"I find that musically, looking back, I have learned much more from those relationships, people I have bumped into that I have admired, that's the way I feel musically I have learned most in life."

John Williams

"He wanted me to make that beautiful Segovia sound and spent a lot of time on hand position and being relaxed. He also wanted no unnecessary hand movement. He taught about control of tone color and that technique is not about speed, but is for control of dynamics."

John Williams (about his father)

"Guitarists are among the worst sight-readers I've come across. Julian (Bream) and I are both dead average sight-readers by orchestral standards, but among guitarists, we are outstanding! This is an area of the guitar that has been poorly taught up until recently".

John Williams

“I never picked up a guitar until I heard Elvis Presley”.

John Lennon

“I don’t read music. I don’t write it. So I wander around on the guitar until something starts to present itself.”

James Taylor

"I just play, just you know, If I just sit

down with the guitar and just do whatever for, you know, an half an hour or an hour whatever. That's pretty much, that should do it for me."

Slash

"That's one of the cool things about going to local bars - seeing what people are doing and jamming with them. I'm a huge advocate of jamming with others; you learn a lot. So I love to go and do that - even if people wipe the stage up with you. There's always something new to learn."

Slash

"I like the Pretenders' James Honeyman-Scott, the Cars' Elliot Easton, who is one of the best lead players of the last 25 years, Joe Walsh, who's one of the best rock and roll guitar players of all time and the Sex Pistols' Steve Jones. I'm also a fan of Elvis Presley's guitarist Scotty Moore and Surf-Rock guitarist Dick Dale. I shouldn't forget David Lindley, who played with Jackson Browne for years. It might surprise some people to hear me say it, but the dude is incredible."

Slash

"I dedicated all the time I had to it. The ten-hour workout was just what I put in the magazine at the time, but for me it was every waking moment."

Steve Vai

"If you want to be a virtuoso on the instrument that's how to do it, ruthless and exacting practice routines."

Steve Vai

"A good solo is like a book. It will start out in a phrase, it will go on in paragraphs, and then it will have a great ending."

Steve Vai

"It seemed to me that no other instrument could express the voicings of a series of moody chords better than a guitar. Bruce Welch showed how beautifully this could be done"

Pete Townshend (in `The Story of The Shadows.')

"Music doesn't lie. If there is something to be changed in this world, then it can only happen through music."

Jimi Hendrix

“Sometimes you want to give up the guitar, you'll hate the guitar. But if you stick with it, you're gonna be rewarded.”

Jimi Hendrix

"I'd like to get something together - like a Handel, Bach, Muddy Waters, flamenco type of thing. If I could get that sound, I'd be happy"

Jimi Hendrix

"The Grand Ole Opry used to come on, and I used to watch that. They used to have some pretty heavy cats, heavy guitar players."

Jimi Hendrix

“Whatever you’ve learned becomes truly useful to you only once it has become second nature. Speed is a by-product of accuracy.”

Guthrie Govan (contributor W. S. Hunter)

“Except for a few guitar chords, everything I’ve learned in my life that is of any value I’ve learned from women.”

Glenn Frey

"Rhythm guitar is like vanilla extract in cake. You can't taste it when it's there, but you know when it's left out."

Irving Ashby

"I practice more than ever, mostly scales and arpeggios ... and anything I can't do. "

Julian Bream

"The best quote I can offer came from Julian Bream who for me was the greatest musician ever to take the guitar as his first instrument. I was at his home directing his life story DVD for *Music On Earth.* I asked about practice and he replied, "I'm retired now so the practice is down to just 4 hours." He had a dedicated shed in the garden where he sat every day and did what needed to be done. His recorded legacy is a gift to the world."

All the best

Paul Balmer,

Author 'The Haynes Guitar Manuals'

"I'm pretty basic as far as technique is concerned. I don't use many gadgets, and I like the sound my guitar makes, anyway."

Brian May

“I'm glad there are a lot of guitar players pursuing technique as diligently as they possibly can, because it leaves this whole other area open to people like me.”

Richard Thompson

"Wes Montgomery played impossible things on the guitar because it was never pointed out to him that they were impossible."

Ronnie Scott

"I don't want you to play me a riff that's going to impress Joe Satriani. Give me a riff that makes a kid want to go out and buy a guitar and learn to play."

Ozzy Osbourne

"We don't like their sound, and guitar music is on the way out."

Decca Recording Company rejecting the Beatles, 1962

"I use heavy strings, tune low, play hard, and floor it. Floor it. That's technical talk."

Stevie Ray Vaughan

"I kept listening, kept going to see people, kept sitting in with people, kept listening to records. If I wanted to learn somebody's stuff, like with Clapton, when I wanted to learn how he was getting some of his sounds, which were real neat, I learned how to make the sounds with my mouth and then copied that with my guitar."

Stevie Ray Vaughan

Les Paul and Mary Ford had just had big chart hits with *Mockingbird Hill* and *How High The Moon.* Les runs into one of his jazz cronies (it was someone well known but I forget the guy's name).

"How ya doing?", Les asks.

"Terrible", the jazzman responds. "Can't get a decent gig that pays nowadays. How do *you* do it?"

Les says, "Would you play 'Mockingbird Hill'?"

"Not on a bet!", snorts the jazz guy.

"Well, that's why we're eating and you're starving."

Les Paul (in the "Chasing Sound" documentary)

Author's note: I'm pretty sure it was Miles Davis.

“The people you’re playing for work all day. They don’t go to music schools and study harmony. They pay their dough, they come to listen. If they don’t understand what you’re doing they walk out. What are you supposed to do, tie ‘em to a chair with a rope while you explain you’re performing great music?”

Les Paul (from the book: Les Paul: An American Original by Mary Alice Shaughnessy)

A friend of mine attended a Robert Conti (jazz guitarist) seminar. During the seminar somebody remarked about how a

> lot of great jazz guitarists seem to come from back East, from places like Philadelphia, Pittsburg and the like. Mr. Conti's two word response was, "Long Winters!"
>
> *(contributor yettoblaster)*

There was a quote that I was trying to remember, and I'm going to massacre it. I believe it was Chet Atkins and another guitar player that was watching either Hank Garland or Grady Martin. The guy turned to Chet Atkins and said,

> "Well that didn't sound too hard. I could play that."

Chet turned to him and said,

> "Of course you can, you just had him show you how to do it."

Something along those lines. Maybe someone can come up with the correct quote.

(contributor banjoman)

> I read somewhere once about two guitarists sitting around backstage and playing for each other as guitarists often do. One of them was playing one of Lenny Breau's arrangements of a song

and the other listened appreciatively. When the guy finished the song his friend said,

"That's really nice but you can't make any money playing that stuff. You know what sells? What sells is when you play something that a fourteen year old kid will hear and say, 'I can play that!'

(contributed by The Norm)

"The whole story behind 'Eruption' is unusual. It wasn't even supposed to be on the album. I showed up early one day and started to warm up because I had a gig on the weekend and I wanted to practice my solo guitar spot.

Our producer, Ted Templeman, happened to walk by and he asked, 'What's that? Let's put it on tape!' So I took one pass at it and they put it on the record. I didn't even play it right. There's a mistake at the top end of it. To this day whenever I hear it I always think, 'Man, I could've played it better'. I think they put it there because it was different, but I'm not really sure."

Eddie Van Halen

"Most beginners want to learn lead guitar because they think it's cool, consequently, they never really develop good rhythm skills. And since most of a rock guitarists time is spent playing rhythm, it's important to learn to do it well. Learning lead should come after you can play solid backup and have the sound of the chords in your head."

Eddie Van Halen

"I think I got the idea of tapping watching Jimmy Page do his "Heartbreaker" solo back in 1971. He was doing a pull-off to an open string and I thought, wait a minute, open string ... pull off. I can do that, but what if I use my finger as the nut and move it around ?" I just kind of took it and ran with it."

Eddie Van Halen

"Eventually you'll take the phrases and rhythm patterns you've copped and begin to put your own mark on them."

Eddie Van Halen

The one thing I do have is good ears. I don't mean perfect pitch, but ears for picking things up. I developed my ear through piano theory, but I never had a guitar lesson in my life, except from Eric Clapton off of records."

Eddie Van Halen

"The hell with the rules. If it sounds right, then it is."

Eddie Van Halen

"Playing scales is like a boxer skipping rope or punching a bag. It's not the thing in itself; it's preparatory to the activity."

Barney Kessel (from Jazz Guitar)

"I don't like to go into the studio with all the songs worked out and planned before hand. You've got to give the band something to use its imagination on as well. That can make a very ordinary song come alive into something totally different - the X-factor - which is the feel. It's so important in rock and roll."

Keith Richards

"I started playing jazz by slowing down Tal Farlow records and analyzing his runs."

Lenny Breau (from Jazz Guitar)

"When you strum a guitar you have everything - rhythm, bass, lead and melody."

Dave Gilmour

"It's hard to describe, because on one hand you want your solo to be spontaneous. On the other hand, I feel a good guitar solo should be somewhat of a composition in itself. So, you sort of toggle back and forth between the concept of trying to initiate flow and composing. I think it's a combination of both."

Jeff 'Skunk' Baxter

"I think people overemphasize the importance of gear in their search for tone. Your sound comes from how you pick and dampen the strings, and from your attack as much as anything."

Eric Johnson

"It's the opportunity to play something completely different, responding to what happened just before you started to play, and I love that."

Larry Carlton

“I want to figure out how I can make the most important statement with the least amount of information, so I don’t run out of ideas by the time I get to my second or third chorus.”

Larry Carlton

"People ask me to describe how I play, and the most obvious answer is that I'm a jazz-influenced guitar player. But I'm not a jazz guitar player. Wes Montgomery was a jazz guitarist, Joe Pass was a jazz guitarist."

Larry Carlton

"Back in the day in my teens I was listening to Joe Pass and Wes Montgomery a lot; before that I was listening to what I would call now the more 'simple' jazz players (but still very valid), like Barney Kessell or Johnny Smith. I learnt a lot of voicings from Johnny Smith records. Now I listen to the old blues players; that's what you'd hear in my house if there was music on. It would be Albert Collins or Albert King. "

Larry Carlton

"The biggest difference between me and other guitar players is that I don't use effects to color my guitar parts, I create guitar parts using effects. They're a crucial part of what I do (but) I don't consider effects a crutch, they're part of the art."

The Edge

"We're all about trying to play better every night, not just singing hit songs ... we ad lib, and every night there's jamming .. it's almost like the Grateful Dead meets Buck Owens some nights, because we'll go off on little adventures and sometimes we do crash the bus!"

Brad Paisley

"Elvis Presleys' first album had more energy and more enthusiasm than any other album at the time - when it was released it just blew everything else out. It changed the whole landscape of music."

Brian Setzer

"Guitarists shouldn't get too riled up about all of the great players that were left off of 'Rolling Stone Magazines' list of the Greatest Guitar Players of all Time'. Rolling Stone is published for people who read the magazine because they don't know what to wear."

Joe Satriani

“I write the songs first and in most cases teach myself the technique second.”

Joe Satriani

"The appearance of Mr. Segovia is not that of the trumpeted virtuoso. He is rather the dreamer or scholar in bearing, long hair, eyeglasses, a black frock coat and neckwear of an earlier generation. He seats himself, thoughtfully, places his left foot on its rest, strikes a soft chord, then bends over his guitar and proceeds to play like the poet and master he is of the instrument."

New York Times , Jan. 9, 1928

"I don't use all my fingers, I can play chords that way but to me it sounds sloppy, I don't like the sound that I get. Joe Pass does it very well, but he uses more of a classical technique. Sometimes I use a finger and the pick for pairs of notes, together or alternately. Lenny Breau plays a harmonic under the chord, he showed me how to do it but I don't do it too well. By making the harmonic on the fourth or fifth string, the bottom voice moves up an octave in between the other notes, where it wouldn't be possible to finger them. He gets a very good close harmony sound that way. He uses a thumb pick all the time, so that makes it easier for him and he plays fast with it."

Tal Farlow (from Jazz Guitar)

"Joao Gilberto on guitar could read a newspaper and sound good."

Miles Davis

"As far as being a 'player's player', you've only got to go to Nashville or Argentina, and you can forget about it. The world is full of amazing guitar players, and you know it, and I know it. It's a humbling experience."

Mark Knopfler

“I think of improvising as composing - for me it's all about playing melodies. When I improvise, there's not a lot of real thinking going on, per se. It's more like riding a wave. and I know how to stand on the board."

Robben Ford

"Don't be afraid to screw up! One of the key issues to learning is making mistakes. If you're not making mistakes, you're probably not having a very good time."

Robben Ford

"My policy is not how fast you play, it's not how much you play but it's what you play and where you play it ... play for the commercial side of the music ... the word I still use today is `simplicity'. It is so important that you use simplicity in your playing and in your music."

James Burton

"What is so important is that you play for the artist and for the record and for the song. Everything else falls into place. My solo has to be a complement to the singer and the song."

James Burton

"Until you learn to play what you want to hear, you're barking up the wrong tree."

Billy Gibbons

"I too once believed in the heavier gauge string as a superior tone source. However, thanks to the graciousness of B.B. King, I learned that a lighter-gauge string offers superior playing comfort. Try it, you may like it."

Billy Gibbons

“The whole idea is that if you turn your amp up to ten, you should still be able to play at a whisper. You’ve got to learn to control with your hands.”

Michael Bloomfield

"My audience has developed so that they come to listen and are quiet, Thus I can work in a limited volume range and explore all the subtleties that can happen, which is my favorite part of the music."

Kenny Burrell (from Jazz Guitar)

"Surrender your whole being into a note, and gravity disappears. With one chord, John Lee Hooker could tell you a story as deep as the ocean."

Carlos Santana

"A long apprenticeship is the most logical way to success. The only alternative is overnight stardom, but I can't give you a formula for that."

Chet Atkins

"It takes a lot of devotion and work, or maybe I should say play, because if you love it, that's what it amounts to. I haven't found any shortcuts, and I've been looking for a long time."

Chet Atkins

"Everyone has their own sound, and if you're heard enough, folks will come to recognize it. Style however, is a different thing. Try to express your own ideas. It's much more difficult to do, but the rewards are there if you're good enough to pull it off."

Chet Atkins

"The music you make is shaped by what you play it on ... if you feel that you're not getting enough out of a song, change the instrument - go from an acoustic to an electric or vice versa, or try an open tuning ... do something to shake it up."

Mark Knopfler

"Although one can get very clever at home, progress comes a lot quicker if you step into a room with other people and start playing. "

Steve Howe

"I'm not conscious of the speed. It's not my motive. My motive is displaying a voice through the fingerboard ... it can get to the point where I don't have control over what I am playing. I never end the gig until I can't sing anymore."

Alvin Lee

"All around it would have to be Eddie Cochran, because it wasn't just music with him; it was his guitar playing, his look, his singing.

I'd say that, all things considered, he's probably my favorite "cat" of all time."

Brian Setzer

"We could play two improvised lines at the same time and it would come out as if someone had stayed up all night and written it out. It's uncanny - the involvement, the harmonization, the counterpoint - the kind of stuff we would get into."

Herb Ellis (on his musical relationship with Joe Pass)

"Once we played at the Fillmore opposite The Cream. Eric Clapton was there and he played his ass off that night. Another guitar player who had a tremendous influence on my life was Howard Roberts. I'd listened to a lot of Tal Farlow, Johnny Smith and Kenny Burrell, and I was certainly into those guys, but I was awestruck at the intensity and fire in Howards' guitar playing. For me, it became a roadmap."

Jeff 'Skunk' Baxter

"My instrumentals try to create some of the basic feelings of human interaction, like anger and joy and love ... with Jessica, I couldn't quite find it, then my little daughter, Jessica, crawled into the room, and I just started playing to her, that's why I named it after her. I came up with that melody using just two fingers as a sort of tribute to Django. In general writing a good instrumental is very fulfilling because you've transcended language and spoken to someone with a melody."

Dickey Betts

"People who love jazz musicians love us when we play what we want to play and we're starving. But as soon as you commercialize your sound like Wes Montgomery did, the jazz fans and the critics are down on you!"

George Benson (from Jazz Guitar)

"My stepfather had an electric guitar. He went to his pawn store one day to get a guitar and an amp, and I couldn't understand what I was hearing. All afternoon, I just sat against the amp and let it reverberate through me. Something must have stuck."

George Benson

"Duane Allman inspired the group to explore the extended jam format that was already a staple of the Allman Brothers act. Moreover, his ferocious slide playing motivated Clapton to turn in some of the finest guitar performances of his career."

Bobby Whitlock (on "Derek and the Dominoes" making the "Layla and other Assorted Love Songs" album)

"The hardest studio music to play is Tom & Jerry cartoons. The music makes absolutely no sense, as music. You can't get into hearing it. There's nothing to hear except, 'bleep!, blop! scratch!' and it comes fast. Everything's first take. That'll change the way you look at life!"

Howard Roberts (from Jazz Guitar)

"Playing live is about going for it. You should see a bunch of people trying out stuff, actually performing, instead of learning the record and recreating it note for note. I can't play the show the same way every night. I really need to be in a creative environment, every night or I'll go nuts. My manager accuses me of singing just long enough to get me to my next guitar solo, which is true."

Brad Paisley

"Charlie Christian had no more impact on my playing than Django Reinhardt or Lonnie Johnson. I just wanted to play like him. I wanted to play like all of them. All of these people were important to me. I couldn't play like any of them, though."

B.B. King

"I first met Jimmy Page in London in 1961, and he was listening to James Burton, Scotty Moore and Cliff Gallup with Gene Vincent, as was I. These were the rock and roll guys who really sparked our interest in the guitar, and later we delved into other things and went different directions. During my time with Eric Clapton, we talked about what we'd listened to early on, and he was a huge fan of Chuck Berry and Jerry Lee Lewis."

Albert Lee

"When I heard Apache by the Shadows, that was it! Then there was a guitar player named Steve Gordon, he was "the player" in town. I still remember him saying to me 'Is there any reason you're not using your little finger?"

Ray Flacke

"And what happened was, it's the same thing an older, more successful writer of fiction might say to a student: write about what you know. And what I knew of course, I knew jazz, but I also knew country, blues and some rock and roll. And that came out."

Larry Coryell (from Jazz Guitar)

"Over the years I hope I've become more of a musician and less of a guitarist."

Larry Coryell (from Jazz Guitar)

"There was nothing that I ever did, no conscious effort to do one kind of behavior or another, I can't explain what it was, but I can explain that the thinking of the time was that we didn't want to emulate our heroes. That wasn't kosher. 'Don't try to play the old cliches, play like yourself' - that's what people were saying."

Larry Coryell (from Jazz Guitar)

"Aqualung was a difficult and very tense album to record. While I was playing the solo, Jimmy Page walked into the control room and started waving. I thought, should I wave back and mess up the solo or should I just grin and carry on ? I just grinned."

Martin Barre

"He was Jimi Hendrix! He didn't sound like anybody else but himself. He was like Charlie Parker in his way of playing, he played well, he was a person that made waves. When you heard Jimi Hendrix you knew it was Jimi Hendrix, he introduced himself in his instrument... You know, many radio stations play records and a lot of the times they don't call out the names who you just listened to, but when they play Jimi Hendrix, you don't have to tell me. You know it's Jimi Hendrix."

B.B. King

“We all have idols. Play like anyone you care about but try to be yourself while you’re doing so.”

B. B. King

"The more you know, the less you know. I don't feel like I know shit anymore, but I love it."

Mike Stern

"If I'm going to buy a new guitar, I take it to a good 'hot' room, like a tiled bathroom, and listen to the wood. If tone comes off the neck, you can bet it's gonna sound beautiful through an amp."

Dickey Betts

"When I joined the trio, it was as if I was capable of driving a sports car at 60, but Ray Brown and Oscar Peterson just kept pressing the pedal down, and I was trying to control the car at 80!"

Barney Kessel (from Jazz Guitar)

"Charlie Christian showed me a lot, and was a great help, but even then, I realised that if I was going to make it, it was no use copying Charlie."

Barney Kessel (from Jazz Guitar)

"Sound is what drives my solos, not verbal concepts, I never think, 'I'm going to use a Lydian Dominant scale and then go up a half-step', even though that might be exactly what I end up doing."

John Scofield

"One thing people always ask me is 'How do you play outside?' I have no idea how to teach that, but when I was discussing this with our bass player Jesse Murphy, he said 'tell them to go cliff diving'. In other words, when you're jamming, you have to take risks if you want to find new sounds."

John Scofield

"Ritchie Blackmore was a huge early influence on me, but after that I had to find my own way. Johann Sebastian Bach was probably the most influential guy ever on me then Vivaldi, Beethoven and eventually Paganini. All of a sudden I was thinking in all these other areas, instead of blues riffs."

Yngwie Malmsteen

"I would urge a young player to listen to Charlie Christians' sense of time. I'll never forget listening to my father and Tal Farlow playing Christians' 'Solo Flight' backstage at a gig. That's when it hit me how big of an effect Christian had on jazz guitar. 'Solo Flight' was like the gospel."

John Pizzarelli

"In 1938 I went out to Tulsa, Oklahoma to see Bob Wills and the Texas Playboys perform. After the set, a bunch of musicians were sitting around talking, and I remember seeing this young black fellow standing around. He came over and asked if I had an extra pick. I gave him one, and then he asked for my autograph. I asked him if he played. He said 'yes' and began to pick. I'll never forget what I said - 'My God, you're good!' That was the first time I met Charlie Christian. As a guitarist Charlie was simply the best around. He had a way of getting on one note and driving it right into the ground. I figured if you're going to be great, you've got to play a lot of notes, right? Not Charlie - he'd hit one note and he'd own it."

Les Paul

"Scotty Moore plays one of the first really amazing riffs in rock history on Heartbreak Hotel with Elvis Presley. It was dangerous, it scared everybodys parents, which was part of the attraction then as it still is now. It totally blindsided me and made me want to get a guitar and do that."

Roger McGuinn

"My ex-wife was trying to be nice once, so she took me to a concert in Los Angeles. I went with her to Symphony Hall, and the orchestra was playing. When the show started, the spotlight was sharp on this one man, Andres Segovia, and he had a sombrero on and his guitar propped up like this and, oh man . He was a master !

I really heard it. That one guitar sounded like a whole orchestra to me."

B.B. King

"The beautiful thing about learning is nobody can take it away from you."

B.B. King

"What I think I do is to relate any new material to how similar it is to something else. The closest that I can come up with something that's already in my experience, the easier it becomes. All I have to do then is remember where it differs, like relating a chord sequence that comes from some other tune, or several different tunes, or maybe parts of them and then work it from there."

Tal Farlow (from Jazz Guitar)

"Listening is the key to everything good in music."

Pat Metheny

"It's interesting to see how acoustic guitars are emerging as a primary instrument once again. It reminds me very much of what Jim Messina and I were doing back then. You can't get too far away from an acoustic guitar."

Kenny Loggins

"Jeff Beck is compelled by his inner artistic drive to keep evolving the instrument. He'll use the whammy bar with the volume knob and the tone control all at the same time - creating harmonics that no human being should be able to hit."

Steve Vai

“Lots of kids when they get their first instrument hammer away at it but they don't realise there are so many levels of dynamics with a guitar.

You can play one note on a guitar and it really gets to people if it is the right note in the right place played by the right person.

Gary Moore

~~~~~~~
~~~~~~~

There was an occasion when Django Reinhardt met Andres Segovia. Django played for the Spanish classical maestro a short jazz crepuscule on his Selmer guitar.

When Django finished, Segovia, dazzled by the piece, asked for a transcription. Django, who didn't read music at all, laughed and explained that it was merely an improvisation, something that Segovia probably would not have understood.

This was fused with his prodigious ability to play anything he heard in his head and a technique that permitted him to execute the ideas instantaneously.

I excerpt here an observation made some time ago by the British composer, Constant Lambert who said,

> "He (Django) swallowed and digested the guitar long ago. Now he is a Ventriloquist."

~~~~~~~

One of my great favourite players is Jim Hall. Jim has so much to say about his approach to playing that he gets his own little section.

"Many guys' solos sound the same. They play on the chord changes rather than improvise on the tune itself. The melody gives you just all that much more to play off."
~~~~~~~

"Lyrics can act as a source of ideas for improvising, too."

"Sometimes it's fun to do that - play a cliche and maybe make something out of it - but I try to keep the solo sounding like it was just invented."

"Players should force themselves to hear something and then play it, rather than just do whatever comes under the fingers."

"I try to make my playing sound as fresh as possible by not relying on set patterns. When I practice, I often tie off some of the strings with rubber bands to force myself to look at the fingerboard differently."

"I guess I sound more reflective because I try to develop a solo compositionally."

"I don't mean to knock bebop, but playing through chord changes one certain way can be a trap. Imitation can be carried too far. That's why you hear so many young sax players who sound like John Coltrane. I'm sure he didn't mean for that to happen."

"I think it's more important to look at paintings than to listen to the way somebody plays bebop lines."

"Many guys, including some well-known artists, play solos that are too long. They could have gotten it all said in 32 or 64 bars."

"It does seem difficult at times. The travelling is hard. And I thought that drinking had something to do with being a musician, but when I decided to quit and went to AA meetings, I found the guys there felt the same thing about their jobs."

"Sometimes travelling makes me so tired I actually feel crazy. Slow practice usually helps if I have time to be alone with the guitar."

"I've been to hear friends at places that were so noisy I actually got angry. The owners seem more interested in selling drinks than in presenting the music well."

"I've started to use a chorus on a couple of tunes. Pat Metheny is really into that kind of stuff. I played a concert with him and he had so much electronic stuff, the stage looked like Mission Control."

"Being able to take music off of a piece of paper is important because that's how music is communicated; however, it isn't everything."

"I have nothing but questions - and that's the truth."

~~~~~~~~
~~~~~~~~

7 When is a fake not a fake? that is the question.

The answer surely is, `only when it's made out to be real.'

It's widely known and acknowledged that much of the guitar playing we hear on recordings wasn't actually played by the artistes themselves - but it's not `fake' unless they try to deceive us by pretending that it was.

Bringing in competent session guys not only guarantees a good result but saves studio time and money. It's often done for expediency rather than because the band's guitarist can't play - after all, he'll have to play the part on live gigs.

Similarly, Les Paul's ground-breaking work with multi-track recording wasn't intended to fool anyone. Les was rightly proud of his technical achievements and was a fine guitarist both live and in the studio.

It does get a little more complicated however when the artist is accused of fraud as in the case of Bay Area tech-death band `Rings of Saturn' who were accused (by their ex-drummer) of recording an album at half-speed to make it easier to play.

The band responded with a statement:

> "Our studio engineer from Mayhemeness Recording Studios for both Embryonic Anomaly, and Dingir, has already made a statement saying that everything found on both our albums is in fact legit and recorded in full time".

The recording engineer owned up to a lot of `punch ins', tempo quantization and copying and pasting but insisted that the recording speed was genuine.

The issue of just how much studio trickery can be justified is a discussion for another day but I note that the band do perform live so maybe it was just a case of sour grapes.

~~~~~~~~

My own experience of such scenarios is limited but here's one little story you may find interesting.

> "The Spotniks used to do this incredibly fast stuff like `Orange Blossom Special' and we used to really kill ourselves .... make our fingers bleed, trying to play it. They did a lot of stuff which I was struggling to play, and then I discovered that they were speeding up the tapes to be able to play that fast."
>
> *Brian May*

And Brian wasn't the only one to smell a rat.
~~~~~~~~

THE `SPECIAL' GUITAR

On February 16 1963, we were asked to play support at the Strand Palais, Walmer, to the Spotnicks, a Swedish instrumental group who had been enjoying quite a measure of chart success during the past few months.

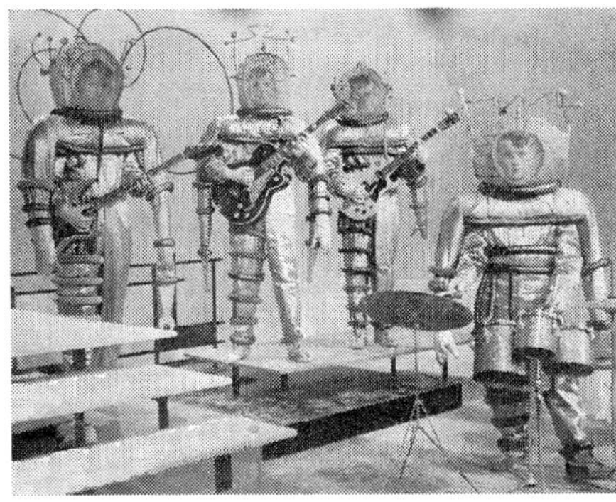

Their gimmick was to wear 'space suits'. In their publicity photos they were shown wearing the bulky, padded outfits complete with boots and huge perspex helmets and the suits, because they weren't exactly the most appropriate attire for going out to play drums or guitar in, had strategically placed holes for their real arms to poke through!

The Spotnicks had first hit the charts in June the previous year with a version of *'Orange Blossom Special'*, a classic bluegrass-style train song from way back. The tune comprises a simple verse, usually sung, and an instrumental section which gives players a chance to show off their skills. Played over a simple three-chord accompaniment, I very much doubt that there was ever an exact tune for the instrumental section - I've heard dozens of versions and no two have been quite the same. It's almost always played at a fair lick however, so generally speaking, a player will choose notes and phrases that suit his instrument, which partly explains why fiddle players, guitarists, harmonica players etc. tend to play slightly different tunes.

The Spotnicks' version was the exception to this rule. The tune they played was incredibly difficult on guitar, especially for alternate picking with a plectrum. We were very suspicious, the more so because their recording had a kind of Les Paul 'speeded-up tape' sound quality about it. We had struggled to learn their arrangement and eventually, feeling we'd got close enough to give it a shot, had taken to playing it at gigs for the past few months where it proved very popular, particularly with other musicians who, depending on various factors, would either be blown away or would stand there taking the piss, hoping to put you off!

But tonight of course we wouldn't play the tune and all would soon be revealed. We played our first set and left the stage. After a big build up, the Spotnicks came on. Not to beat about the bush, they were a huge disappointment. The suits they wore were nothing like those in the publicity shots - more like shiny grey overalls - and of course they couldn't do a gig inside the helmets! The playing was mediocre and, worst of all, they didn't play their big hit *Orange Blossom Special.* The crowd shouted for it, we shouted for it - all to no avail. At the end of their set, their tour manager who spoke some English, came forward to apologise and explain. It seems the problem was that they needed a `special guitar' to play it on and unfortunately it had been left behind in Sweden! Oh well, that's all right then.

Bass player Pete Inwood turned to me. `Well, we've got to do it now', he said and the rest of the band agreed. When we returned to the stage for our second set, Pete announced to the audience that by a stroke of luck we happened to have with us a `special guitar' that would enable us to play *Orange Blossom Special* and that if only we'd known about the Spotnicks' problem we'd have let them borrow it. I remember making even more cock-ups than usual but nobody seemed to notice and the audience gave a us a huge ovation. After that we could do no wrong and the rest of our set went from strength to strength. When the audience finally let us off the stage, the Spotnicks manager rushed up to see us. He told us in glowing terms that we would be 'huge in Sweden'. He wanted to sign us up there and then but we told him we'd decided not to give up the day jobs to work with a guy who couldn't even be trusted to pack the right guitars!

(Just for the record, the only guitarist I've ever seen play the Spotnicks' version absolutely spot on at a live gig was a guy called Ricky Harding. He was with a group called the Crestas at the Empress Ballroom, Folkestone. He played it on a beautiful Gretsch White Falcon and was superb).

Mick Morris (`The Special guitar!' from 'Don't Give up The Day Job!)

8 Bucking the system

Music and society have always been intimately related. But because music not only reflects but also influences social conditions, including the factors that either facilitate or impede social change, it has often had a difficult relationship with authority. And it's not hard to see why. The problem for those in authority is that music encourages the sharing of values between cultures, crossing borders and transcending issues that those in power want to control.

Music promotes the development and maintenance of individual, group, cultural and even national identities. Throughout history this has been recognised and in many societies those in power have attempted to control music.

Despite this, musicians themselves would go to great lengths to get around the obstacles put in their way by society.

~~~~~~~

> "A lot of times, I was the only white musician in a band, but usually I felt privileged to be there."
>
> *Jim Hall*
~~~~~~~

In the USA, in clear breach of racial segregation laws, many black and white musicians seized every opportunity to play together. One such early collaboration was that between guitarists Eddie Lang and Lonnie Johnson who first recorded together in 1929.

The idea to team Lang and Johnson originated with T. J. Rockwell, artist manager for OKeh Records. It was also his idea to mask the fact that the 26-year-old Lang was white by arranging for the labels on the American releases of their original records to be credited to `Lonnie Johnson and Blind Willie Dunn.' Lonnie and `Blind Willie' embarked on a series of guitar duets that would exert a profound influence on jazz guitar, then in its formative stage.

Eddie, as `Blind Willie Dunn', also recorded with several blues singers initially showcasing his guitar skills on Alma Henderson's `You Can't Have It Unless I Give It to You". Other dates found him paired with African-American blues singers such as Victoria Spivey, Eva Taylor, and Gladys Bentley on her "How Much Can I Stand?" and "Wild Geese Blues". He also recorded with his own mixed-race group `Blind Willie Dunn and his Gin Bottle Four'. Lonnie Johnson fondly recalled Eddie Lang in an interview for the 1955 book, `Hear Me Talkin' to Ya'.

"I well remember Eddie Lang. He was the nicest man I ever worked with. Eddie and I got together many a time in the old OKeh record studios in New York, and we made many sides together with just two guitars. Eddie was a fine man. I've never seen a cat like him since. He could play guitar better than anyone I know. And I've seen plenty in my day. At that time I was working for the Columbia record people in New York. That's all I did - just make sides. But the sides I made with Eddie Lang were my greatest experience."

~~~~~~~~

Although racial segregation persisted, music was one area in which authority was gradually losing the battle.

Another early inter-racial collaboration was that between guitarist George Barnes and blues artist Big Bill Broonzy. On March 1, 1938, Broonzy and Barnes got together to record two tracks, `Sweetheart Land' and `It's a Low-Down Dirty Shame'.

The session, produced by Lester Melrose in Chicago, is notable for being the first ever recording of an electric guitar.
~~~~~~~~

The following year, Charlie Christian became featured electric guitarist with Benny Goodman's otherwise all white band.

But whilst there were signs of at least some progress in the USA, elsewhere, things were moving in the opposite direction.

DJANGO'S WAR

In 1930's Germany, the newly elected Nazi government was set on overturning what it saw as the dangerous cultural excesses allowed under the previous administration. Music that was regarded as 'racially impure' was banned. Black artists were banned from the radio and from giving concerts, American music was banned and serious penalties were introduced for those caught listening to it.

But though the German state denigrated jazz, musicians, swing dancers and many Nazi soldiers loved it. The solution the Nazis came up with was to introduce `rules for jazz performers'. As Jews, Gypsies and Black people - groups targeted by the Nazis - were also the primary innovators of jazz music, the rules included such requirements as `no gloomy Jewishy lyrics," `no Negroid excesses in tempo', and `no hysterical rhythmic reverses characteristic of the barbarian races.'

In September 1939 when World War II broke out, Django Reinhardt and Stephane Grapelli were on tour with the quintet in England. Reinhardt immediately made his way back to France, taking a train from London to Dover, catching the ferry and leaving Grappelli to spend the entire duration of the war in Britain.

Django spent the winter of 1939 playing in Jimmy's Bar in Montparnasse. but in spring 1940 the German blitzkrieg led to the speedy fall of France. He fled the city when the Germans occupied Paris

but soon returned, forming a new quintet and even eventually opening a new club, `La Roulotte'.

Two or three times he attempted to leave France after being tipped off that the Nazis were gassing Gypsies and on one occasion he made it to the Swiss border before being captured. He was only released because the commander happened to be a fan of his. The popularity of jazz and Django especially, among German officers, together with the difficulty of implementing the vaguely worded `rules for jazz performers', kept him safe through the years of occupation. The protection in particular of Dietrich Schulz-Köehn, a Luftwaffe officer aka "Doktor Jazz", a great admirer of Django, enabled him to continue to perform during the German occupation, in an era where many European gypsies faced the fatal consequences of racial hatred.

~~~~~~~
~~~~~~~

Meanwhile back in the USA, the political establishment was still doing its best to make things difficult for musicians. In 1953, folk guitarist and banjo player Pete Seeger was among those blacklisted by radio stations for his `un-American views'.

And more than ten years later, it was still necessary on September 11 1964, for John Lennon to announce that The Beatles would not play to a segregated audience in Jacksonville, Florida. City officials relented following his announcement.

The following year, a contract for The Beatles to perform in concert at the Cow Palace in California needed to specify that the band "not be required to perform in front of a segregated audience".

\~\~\~\~\~\~\~

"You didn't know whether Chuck Berry was black or white - it was not a concern."

Keith Richards

That's pretty much as I remember it too, but some people apparently did know and did have concerns.

\~\~\~\~\~\~\~

HAVE THIS ONE ON ME CHUCK

It was our first night in Dallas where we'd gone to see The Cowboys play football. A group of us went to a huge out of town eaterie called The Trail Dust Steak House - one of those places where they serve steaks so huge that if you can eat one it's free. We were having a good time. The food had been superb and the Budweisers were going down well. On the stage the house band was doing a good job of cranking out Lynyrd Skynyrd covers.

From the stage I heard, "Hey folks, we've got a special guest tonight. His name is Mick and he's here all the way from England to play for us". I made my way to the stage and the guy on the microphone handed me his guitar. "What are you gonna do then Mick?", he asked. Good question. I hadn't had time to think about that. Ideally it would be something the audience would recognise and something the band could play without trouble. It would also have to be something I'd still be able to handle when the Budweisers kicked in!

"What about the old Chuck Berry number, 'Johnny B. Goode'", I suggested. His face was a picture. He leaned towards me and turned the microphone away so that the audience wouldn't hear him.

"I'll tell you what Mick, why don't you pick something else". "Say, what about some Jerry Lee Lewis or something, only you can't play any of that ni**er sh*t in here."

I don't know how many thoughts can race through your mind in a split second - but believe me it's a hell of a lot. Here's a small selection of what went through mine as I stood there momentarily lost for words for what seemed like an age but what I was later told was just an instant.

Did I imagine what I thought he just said? I thought about the first time I saw Chuck, how I loved his songs and his guitar playing. I thought about Little Richard and Fats Domino. I thought about the white guys - Elvis, Buddy Holly, Jerry Lee himself - they hadn't felt that way and this was 1990 not 1960. They were a rock and roll band for Christ's sake - where did they think the music came from? I thought about Stevie Ray Vaughan who had died just three months earlier. Stevie had been born and raised in Dallas. Had he experienced this kind of thing?

I was angry and briefly contemplated telling him to shove his telecaster where the sun doesn't shine but then I realised maybe it wasn't him but the audience that laid down the ground rules. Now I love 'Great Balls of Fire' as much as the next man but I knew then I couldn't go along with it. The `tour' would have to be cut short! I muttered something along the lines of, "Sorry pal, but it's Chuck or nothing" and handed him his guitar back. Leaving him to explain to the crowd, I returned to puzzled expressions all round on our table.

Still in a state of disbelief, I tried to explain what had happened. We drank up and left.

Mick Morris (from `Don't Give up The Day Job')

~~~~~~~~
~~~~~~~~

9 Right time, right place - Some happy accidents?

Sometimes it's just a matter of being in the right place at the right time - one man's misfortune can be another's lucky day.

Take the case of Hank Marvin. It's hard to imagine the Shadows without Hank but the job nearly went to Tony Sheridan. Cliff Richard's manager John Foster was looking for a new lead guitarist. He had his heart set on Tony Sheridan but Tony, who had a reputation for always being late, ran true to form and didn't turn up in time.

> "The obvious person was Tony Sheridan but I was still waiting for Tony to arrive when Hank walked in with his guitar. He was as good as I'd been told, and although I'd had my heart set on Tony, I'd have missed the bus home if I hung around any longer so I offered Hank the tour with Cliff and he agreed to do it as long as he could bring his mate Bruce along to play rhythm."
>
> *John Foster - Cliff's then manager (in `The Story of The Shadows.')*

Tony wasn't a bad player by any means, but one thing's certain - the `Shadows' sound' wouldn't have happened if he'd got the job

Tony went to Hamburg in 1960 and was still there when the Beatles arrived the following year. They recorded a number of tracks together for the German Polydor label, one or two of which enjoyed limited chart success, but major stardom continued to elude Tony.

He did have one lucky break though. Before going to Hamburg, he'd been on tour with Eddie Cochran and Gene Vincent. He'd asked if he could ride to the next gig in the car with Eddie and Gene but was told there wasn't room. When the car crashed, Cochran was killed and Vincent seriously injured.

~~~~~~~

Still on the subject of The Shadows, even more incredible is the way that the inimitable sound of the Shadows came about by yet another accident.

Hank had never really been happy with the guitars he'd played - it was very difficult to get a decent guitar in the UK back then - and was looking for a better instrument. Without any doubt, one of the best sounding players around at that time was James Burton. His guitar work on recordings by Ricky Nelson was superbly played and had a great
~~~~~~~

tone. That was the sound Hank was after. Cliff Richard sent for a Fender catalogue.

> "We could see that Buddy Holly's guitar was the Stratocaster and as that was their top-of-the-range model, we assumed that James Burton would also have one."
>
> *Hank Marvin*

This is how Bruce Welch tells the story.

"Cliff, Hank and I had a flat at 100 Marylebone High St. We loved the sound of American records - Gene Vincent, Buddy Holly and especially Rick Nelson, with James Burton on guitar, although we didn't know his name then. We knew this guy played a Fender and so Cliff sent to Santa Ana in California for a brochure, which duly arrived at the flat. We nearly creamed our jeans at that! I remember Mark Knopfler saying that he can remember the smell of the fender brochure and he's right, you can. Anyway, flicking though the pages we came to this flamingo pink, birds-eye maple neck Stratocaster; gold-plated hardware and with the old wobble bar. We presumed that the guy in the Ricky Nelson band played this one - well, he would, wouldn't he, the most expensive guitar in the catalogue. Anyway, back it came and... well, the rest is history and of course James Burton played a Telecaster. As I pointed out to Cliff, there's a letter reproduced in his own authorised biography that says, 'Dear Ray, we've decided to have the Stratocaster. Please send us the red one with the gold-plated parts'.

So the unique sound of the Shadows which was essentially the sound of Hank and his Fender Stratocaster. was itself the result of not just one but two accidents.

~~~~~~~~

Other times, something which turns out really good is the result of a mistake which if rectified would have a produced a different, but not necessarily better, result.

~~~~~~~~

In 1972 Elliott Randall moved from NY to LA and met up with his old session musician friends Walter Becker and Donald Fagen who were working on the first Steely Dan album, “Can’t Buy A Thrill.”

The album already featured Denny Dias and Jeff “Skunk” Baxter on guitars but they didn’t think their work on “Reelin’ in The Years” quite fitted and asked Elliott to play. He turned up at the studio with his '63 Stat (humbucker retrofitted in the neck position) to find the only amp in the studio was an Ampeg SVT 400w bass amp with an 8 x 10 cab. After some discussion, the engineer suggested they mic up the cab, turn the amp right up to get some distortion and wear some ear protection and that is what they did!

They played Elliott the track and he nailed it on take one. Unfortunately, the engineer thought he was just having a run through and hadn't hit the record button so he did another take and that is what appears on the track. Randall felt the second take wasn't as good as the first but they left it at that and the rest, as they say, is history.

(Contributed by Nick Charlesworth)

~~~~~~~~

"A blown-out tube ripped some of the grind from the amplifier, throwing us into a momentary tizzy. The unusual sound led me to play unusually, and the recorded take turned out to be a keeper. Inspiration can come from the most unlikely places. Keep your head on and your ears open."

Billy Gibbons

~~~~~~~~

SHOULD HAVE GONE FOR IT PETE!

"My good friend Pete Inwood and I often used to get together to try out new songs, usually at Pete's parents house. Pete wasn't the only musically inclined member of the family - his twin cousins, Jean and Gloria Harrison, were singers who performed as The Harrison Twins. The girls, who played holiday camps, hotels and small theatres had decided to form a new cabaret act and were looking for a boy to join them singing and playing the guitar. Their agent soon found just the right lad, playing and singing in The Prince of Wales Feathers, a pub on Warren Street in Camden, London.

The new act, called The Highlights, made their debut at the Sunshine Holiday Camp (Mill Rythe Holiday Village) Hayling Island in the summer of 1963.

Occasionally The Highlights would play air bases and army camps in Europe and would drive down to Dover, often staying overnight at Pete's mum and dad's to catch an early morning ferry to France. Pete and I got to know the lad who's name was Ricky (he called himself Ricky Harrison and pretended to be the girls' brother!) and he would sometimes jam with us.

While The Highlights were playing at Butlins, Minehead Ricky became friendly with some other lads who were playing there in an R&B group called The Spectres. Ricky and the band's guitarist singer became particularly good friends and one evening Ricky told Pete the Spectres were going to audition him.

Being a cabaret act, The Highlights played a very different type of material consisting mostly of middle of the road pop songs and Ricky, obviously worried that he wouldn't get the job, asked for help in learning to play in more of an R&B style. Pete in particular spent a lot of time showing Ricky how to play R&B rhythms based on what we'd learned from the way Chuck Berry played, which had already found its way into British rock via bands like the Rolling Stones and other early R&B outfits. I told Pete that instead of giving Ricky free guitar lessons he should just apply for the job himself.

Anyway, it seems to have worked because The Spectres' (who by this time had changed their name to Traffic Jam) manager Pat Barlow invited Ricky to join the group in July 1967. Soon after, Ricky Harrison became Rick Parfitt and Traffic Jam became Status Quo."

Mick Morris (from `Don't Give up The Day Job')

~~~~~~~~
~~~~~~~~

10 Careful with that axe Eugene - Some not so happy accidents

Most bad accidents are caused by people doing really stupid things. Mitch Holder, a protegee of top session guitarist and `Wrecking Crew' member Howard Roberts, tells of a dissonant episode between Roberts and Phil Spector who, as we now know, had a lifelong penchant for playing around with firearms.

~~~~~~~

Roberts, an avid outdoorsman with a fervent respect for guns, recoiled on a recording date when Spector fired his pistol into the ceiling. Roberts left the session, telling Spector, "I just can't do this. I can't stay here. Don't call me again." In Denny Tedesco's documentary, *The Wrecking Crew*, noted session drummer Hal Blaine said, "Howard Roberts was the only person I've ever seen walk out on a date." Holder added, "It wasn't really like Howard to get mad, but he had such respect for firearms."

~~~~~~~

Probably most of the serious accidents to guitar players have resulted from faulty wiring systems. Electric shocks come in all shapes and sizes, ranging from the minor lightning strikes that many of us have experienced to more serious electrical faults which have resulted in injury and in a few cases disaster. Most electrical systems connect one supply conductor to earth (or ground) but if a fault within an electrical device such as an amp, microphone or guitar connects a hot unearthed supply conductor to an exposed conductive surface, like a guitar or mic, anyone touching it while electrically connected to the earth i.e. making contact with the ground will complete the circuit and receive an electrical shock.

~~~~~~~

"Hundreds of kids would pack into Tofts club until the atmosphere became as humid as that of a rain forest. The sweat poured from us and formed pools on the stage. Whether the club had a problem with electrical earthing or whether, more likely, it was down to our ancient Geloso PA amplifier with its quirky Italian electronics, we were lucky to survive our sets at Tofts which were routinely punctuated by the spectacular but painful phenomenon of blue sparks arcing between the microphones and our lips and noses."

Mick Morris (from `Don't Give up The Day Job')

~~~~~~~

Keith Richards got shocked at the Veteran's Memorial Hall in Sacramento, California on December 3rd, 1965. As the Stones launched into "The Last Time" Richards bumped his guitar into a mic stand, ordinarily not a big deal, except this particular stand happened to be ungrounded, creating an electrical surge that unleashed a shower of sparks and left Richards unconscious on the floor.

A writer who was there at the time said,

> "I was right there in the front row, in front of Keith. I saw the blue light (and) I literally saw Keith fly into the air backward. I thought he was dead. I was horrified. We all were. Silence fell over the crowd. They carried him out with oxygen tubes and he was semiconscious."

Richards ultimately pulled out of his ordeal, reportedly thanks to the fact he'd been wearing a pair of new rubber-soled boots, but things looked dicey for a bit, a nearby doctor saying encouragingly,

"Well, they either wake up or they don't."

~~~~~~~~

During his last tour with Uriah Heep, bassist Gary Thain suffered an electric shock at the Moody Coliseum in Dallas, Texas on 15 September 1974, and was seriously injured.

~~~~~~~~

In 1940 while experimenting with various types of wiring, Les Paul electrocuted himself pretty seriously. This required a period of two years recovery which caused him to leave NY completely.

~~~~~~~~

Another very lucky guy is Ace Frehey of Kiss. At a gig on Dec. 12, 1976 at the Civic Center in Lakeland, Florida, Frehley grabbed onto a metal rail to steady himself and in so doing completed an electrical circuit with his guitar. Seized by the current he was initially unable to move but finally broke free and fell several feet onto the stage below.

> "If I hadn't been able to let go, I would have died," Frehey later said, "My life passed in front of my eyes. I knew it for an instant and then I blacked out. I woke up behind the amplifiers."

Shaken, but not seriously hurt, he took a ten-minute break in the dressing room before returning to the stage to a standing ovation and finishing the night's set.

He said, "I can’t play", but the fans started chanting his name and he finished the show saying afterwards, "I had no feeling in my hands. I don’t know how I did it. I guess it was all adrenaline." The experience inspired his song "Shock Me," which became the first track he ever sang on a Kiss album.

~~~~~~~~

Others who have suffered similar shocks but survived them include George Harrison, Nick Lowe and Kelly Jones, singer/guitarist with The Stereophonics.

Lucky escapes for some of us then, but others have not been so fortunate.

In May 1972, Les Harvey, brother of Alex Harvey and guitarist with Stone the Crows, became an honorary, if somewhat little-known, member of the 27 club when he was electrocuted on stage at the Top Rank Ballroom in Swansea by touching a microphone that was not earth-grounded with his wet hands. Harvey was killed and it was found that the earth wire inside the mains plug for the mic amp had come adrift and was touching the live terminal, making the body of the mic live. Les was holding onto the neck of his guitar, which was properly earthed through the amplifier mains plug, with one hand and grabbed hold of the live mic with his other hand. The circuit was then completed and Les died instantly. Negligence on the part of a stage hand was found to be to blame.

~~~~~~~

John Rostill, bassist with The Shadows for seven years, died on November 26, 1973 at his home in Radlett, Hertfordshire, UK, electrocuted by his bass guitar in his home studio. Bruce Welch had called around to Rostill's home to work on some songs and got no reply. When he and John's wife Margaret gained access to the studio they found him dead.
~~~~~~~

In 1976, Keith Relf, former singer for British rhythm and blues band The Yardbirds, died while practicing his electric guitar. He was electrocuted by an improperly grounded amplifier. He had fitted out the basement of his house as a recording studio and this is where he was found on the floor by his son. His guitar was not properly earthed, and although the shock was fairly mild, Keith had been ill and was not fit enough to withstand it.

~~~~~~~~

In November 2014, Agustin Briolini, the young guitarist and lead singer of a popular Argentinian rock band died after getting a massive electric shock as he opened his set to promote the band's first album. Medics rushed to his aid, but after spending an hour trying to revive him, the singer was taken to hospital where doctors pronounced him dead.

It was found that faulty wiring on his microphone had led to his death on stage as he performed at the Theatre of the Sun, in the city of Villa Carlos Paz. He was just 21 years old.

~~~~~~~~

And then of course, some injuries are non-electrical and caused by the instrument itself.

"Nobody f*****g upstages us"

Peter Townshend (after ramming the butt of his guitar into the back of Abbie

Hoffman's head, when Hoffman ran on stage during the Who's set, and made a quick political announcement)

~~~~~~~~

But the prize for the unluckiest men ever to suffer death by electric guitar must surely go to the three guys up next, all of them killed by instruments that weren't even plugged in.

On October 30, 2012, the Forest Hill police department received a frantic phone call from the secretary of the Greater Sweethome Missionary Baptist Church in Forest Hill, Texas. She told them that the pastor, the Rev. Danny Kirk, had been chased into the church by a man who was now attacking him.

When the police arrived, they found the suspect beating Kirk with an electric guitar and used a taser to subdue him. Both men were taken to hospital but Kirk died from his injuries soon after and the suspect was "found unresponsive shortly after being detained" and also pronounced dead. No motive for the killing has ever been established.

~~~~~~~~

On 24 April 2012, Maurice Leray Eckert was also beaten to death with an electric guitar. The crime took place at an apartment complex in southeast Austin, Texas where Eckert had been drinking with his upstairs neighbor, killer 42-year-old Peter Andrew Levay who was sentenced to twenty-five years in prison.

Austin bills itself as the "Live Music Capital of the World." Hmm ...

~~~~~~~~

On Saturday 27 December 2014, a Belfast man was beaten to death with his own guitar. Matthew Goddard was found dead at his house in Chobham Street in east Belfast by a friend who had come round to pick up Christmas presents. Northern Ireland police investigating the murder of Mr Goddard reported that a 'violent and sustained' assault had taken place on Christmas Eve and said the killer had used the victim's own electric guitar in a brutal assault.

~~~~~~~~

11 To absent friends

I'd like to offer my personal apologies to all those whose names should have appeared but for one reason or another didn't.

In particular to the long-forgotten pioneers of the guitar, to the largely anonymous backroom boys of the session world and to the sidemen who often get too little credit for their contributions.

They include many of my personal favourites such as Ken Sykora, Ike Isaacs, Judd Proctor, Denny Wright, Diz Disley and Ollie Halsall (UK), Sacha Distel, Bireli Lagrene (France), Franny Beecher, Oscar Moore, Jimmy Raney (USA) and many more.

Anyway thanks a lot guys. You deserve a book of your own.

MAM

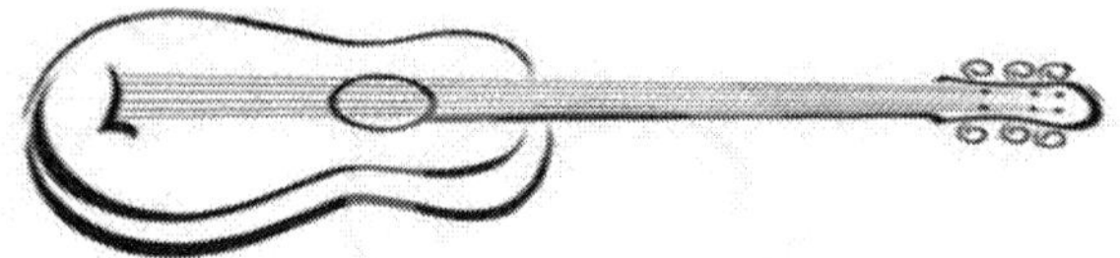

ABOUT THE AUTHOR

Mick Morris was born in the south east of England. He is a guitarist, teacher of the instrument and writer: the author of the *Play Straight Away* guitar tutor, *Don't Give up The Day Job!,* a biographical memoir of his early musical experiences and *The Life of the Limerick.*

He has also contributed articles to music magazines as well as recording several albums of his own. Most of all though he is a guitar aficionado.

~~~~~~~
~~~~~~~

24445780R00122

Printed in Poland
by Amazon Fulfillment
Poland Sp. z o.o., Wrocław